Library of
Davidson College

PHILOSOPHY AND COMMON SENSE
J. David Newell

UNIVERSITY
PRESS OF
AMERICA

Copyright © 1980 by

J. David Newell

University Press of America, Inc.

P.O. Box 19101, Washington, D.C. 20036

All rights reserved

Printed in the United States of America

ISBN: 0-8191-0968-1 (Perfect)

Library of Congress Catalog Card Number: 79-9642

To

my students

past and present

at

Washington College

ACKNOWLEDGEMENTS

I wish to acknowledge the assistance of Washington College in the publication of this book. I am especially grateful to Gertrude Starkey and Leone Eaton for their efficient secretarial services. The manuscript in its present form was typed by Kathi McMillen (MSOS, 407 Washington Avenue, Chestertown, Maryland) and her assistance is gratefully acknowledged. Proofreading assistance was rendered by the staff of MSOS, as well as by my wife Judith. I am also grateful to the publishing houses and authors cited on the first page of each chapter for granting permission (where applicable) to use their materials. Any errors which occur herein are my responsibility.

The Editor

CONTENTS

	INTRODUCTION	1
I.	THE HANDMAID OF LIFE A. K. Rogers	9
II.	THOUGHT AND TEMPERAMENT C. E. M. Joad	15
III.	PRAGMATISM AND COMMON SENSE William James	29
IV.	WHAT IS COMMON SENSE? Thomas Reid	43
V.	THE PHILOSOPHY OF COMMON SENSE Henry Sidgwick	49
VI.	A DEFENCE OF COMMON SENSE G. E. Moore	61
VII.	DEFENDING COMMON SENSE Norman Malcolm	75
VIII.	ORDINARY LANGUAGE AND COMMON SENSE A. D. Woozley	99
IX.	METAPHYSICS AND COMMON SENSE A. J. Ayer	109
X.	THE VALUE OF PHILOSOPHY J. David Newell	131
	SELECTED BIBLIOGRAPHY	143

INTRODUCTION

Philosophy and common sense are indeed very different things and most philosophers would be quick to emphasize the differences between them. The essays in this book, however, deal in a generally positive way with the relationship between philosophy and common sense. In focusing on this relationship, the emphasis is on the connection, if any, between what we ordinarily believe, on the one hand, and what we believe as the result of philosophical investigation, on the other. There is no attempt to develop a "philosophy of common sense," as such, even though certain of the authors represented are themselves inclined to do so. The selections included represent a variety of ways in which we might conceive of the role of the philosopher in dealing with our ordinary understanding of things.

In the first selection, A.K. Rogers argues that philosophy which is divorced from life is formal and barren. Rogers believes that everyone has a philosophy of life in that each person adopts a general attitude or outlook in terms of which he or she views the world. Philosophy proper is a more thorough systematic and objective approach to what we do in our everyday thinking. Philosophy sometimes strays far beyond its position as "the handmaid of life," says Rogers, but it never really loses sight of its relationship to the real world. As the handmaid of life, philosophy takes as its data "the same facts with which science and history, and everyday living deal." The business of philosophy is to deepen and enrich our understanding of the familiar facts and beliefs which we all embrace anyway.

C.E.M. Joad is aware of the fact that this concern about the harmony of philosophy and common sense will not appeal to everyone. The concluding chapter of his Essays on Common-Sense Philosophy, entitled "Thought and Temperament," focuses attention on the notion that

> ...the sort of creed you hold, the philosophic school you belong to, the view you take in purely intellectual matters, is to some extent conditioned by your character as a whole, and by your general outlook on life intellectual, emotional and instinctive.

The influence of temperament on thought for which Joad argues will itself be disputed by some philosophers, but Joad points out that this too is a matter of temperament. Mathematics, logic and certain scientific statements may not be much influenced by one's temperament, but Joad thinks philosophical outlooks surely are. Whether or not the average person can be drawn into the philosophical arena in the first place may well be a matter of temperament. And whether or not, once in the arena, we are concerned to keep our feet on the ground, so to speak, may also be a matter of temperament. We may suggest that, if Joad is right, the quarrel between the metaphysician and the common sense philosopher probably has its roots in the characters and temperaments of each.

An even-tempered individual might try to strike a balance between philosophy and common sense in his assessment of the importance of each. An example of just such an approach is found in the essay by William James entitled "Pragmatism and Common Sense." According to James, we cannot avoid holding a somewhat commonsensical view of the world. Common sense knowledge is "a perfectly definite stage in our understanding of things." It is a stage of knowledge which has grown and developed over centuries of time and at any particular point in human history it supplies man with a sort of equilibrium of thought which counterbalances the onrushing explorations of both science and philosophy. James advocates a certain measure of healthy suspicion of the common sense view, but allows that it stands on equal grounds with scientific and philosophical views. Common sense, science, and critical philosophy are presented by James as "three well-characterized levels, stages, or types of thought about the world we live in." Each stage has its own special function and James does not think we can say that any one of these stages is superior to the other two. Common sense is better for one sphere of life, science for another, and philosophy for still another.

A somewhat more integral connection between philosophy and common sense than that offered by James is presented by Thomas Reid. Reid sees common sense as a gift from God, an inward light having varying degrees of brightness in each individual. It is common sense that makes us eligible for participation in the social and political order, and it is common sense that makes us accountable to others for our conduct. At an even deeper level, this heavenly gift is seen by Reid as that faculty of the human mind which enables us to evaluate the underlying principles of human knowledge. Reid writes,

> All knowledge, and all science, must be built upon principles that are self-evident, and of such principles, every man who has common sense is a competent judge when he conceives them distinctly.

If mankind as a whole is endowed by the Creator with common sense, it follows that the philosopher ought to be prepared to submit his basic principles to the final judgment of the masses. Reid's confidence in the intuitive powers of the average person would seem somewhat extreme. This point is made by Sidgwick in the essay which follows the Reid selection.

It is important to point out that, even though Reid sees common sense as a heavenly gift, the authority he attributes to it does not rest entirely with its alleged divine origins. For common sense, on Reid's view, is the "first born" of human reason. Like most philosophical intuitionists, Reid sees reason as having two distinct, but related, functions: it enables us to discover and apprehend self-evident truths, and it enables us to draw inferences from these truths. But self-evident truths, for Reid, are the "sole province" of common sense. The fundamental beliefs of common sense, then, are entirely in accord with the deliverances of human reason--however refined or sophisticated these deliverances may be.

Reid's common sense philosophy is given further exposition and explanation by Henry Sidgwick in "The Philosophy of Common Sense." Sidgwick thinks Reid should have limited his appeal to the common sense beliefs of generally well-educated persons in the more civilized societies of the world. In particular, the appeal is most legitimately made to the common sense beliefs of the philosopher himself. Sidgwick points out that philosophers themselves, especially when not engaged in philosophical pursuits, usually share certain beliefs about the universe with the ordinary man. As examples of such beliefs, Sidgwick offers our belief in the independent existence of physical objects such as trees and tables, our belief in the existence of mental acts and states of consciousness, our belief that every event must have a cause, and even our belief in the moral rightness or wrongness of certain human actions. The "essential demand" made by Reid (and Sidgwick) is that the philosopher should make his philosophical beliefs consistent with these other beliefs which he holds in common with the rest of mankind. This demand, Sidgwick notes, can be made as much in the name of philosophy as in the name of common sense.

In the selection included here, Sidgwick's conception of the relationship between philosophy and common sense is not fully explored.[1] In other writings Sidgwick takes the view that philosophy is the science of the sciences. The various individual sciences seek to organize and systematize their own principles, methods and conclusions into unified and coherent bodies of knowledge. The separate sciences, in effect, organize, modify and sharpen the beliefs of common sense. Philosophy, in turn, seeks the ultimate unification and harmony of all human knowledge which we have through science and common sense. But, in his Methods of Ethics, Sidgwick notes that the function of the philosopher

> ...is to tell men what they ought to think, rather than what they do think: he is expected to transcend Common Sense in his premises, and is allowed a certain divergence from Common Sense in his conclusions.[2]

Philosophy, then, has the upper hand, on Sidgwick's view, but the philosopher is not thereby granted license to play fast and loose with the established beliefs of science and common sense.

A splendid example of the influence of temperament and character on thought, insisted on by Joad, is found in the philosophy of George Edward Moore. In English Philosophy Since 1900, G.J. Warnock notes that

> Among the immediately operative factors contributing to the decay of Absolute Idealism, special notice should be paid to the character of Moore... He seems to have been, in the first place, entirely without any of the motives that tend to make a metaphysician. He was neither discontented with nor puzzled by the ordinary beliefs of plain men and plain scientists. He had no leanings whatever towards paradox and peculiarity of opinion.[3]

Moore remarked that Sidgwick's "clarity and his belief in common sense were very sympathetic" to him.[4] Moore's sympathies for the common sense view are expressed in his celebrated essay, "A Defence of Common Sense," part of which is reprinted below.

Moore boldly announces a long list of common sense "truisms" which he thinks we all know, with certainty, to be true. These beliefs, which comprise what Moore calls the common sense view of the world, are very similar to the common sense beliefs presented in the Sidgwick reading. Moore thinks that philosophers have generally taken one of three approaches to these common sense beliefs. The second part of the Moore selection contains excerpts from "What is Philosophy?" in which Moore sketches these three philosophical reactions to common sense. The first view tries to add something significant to the common sense view, without denying or contradicting it. As an example of this approach, Moore cites philosophers who append a belief in the existence

of God or the after-life to the common sense view. The
second approach to common sense beliefs is simply to
contradict the beliefs of common sense, as in the case
of philosophers who conclude that time is unreal or
that reality is one indivisible whole. The third approach involves both the contradiction of common sense
and the addition of something to it. Moore cites Berkeley's idealism as an example of this approach. It is
Moore's view that, once we recognize the truth of the
beliefs of common sense, it is the job of the philosopher to provide some sort of adequate analysis of them.

The essay by Norman Malcolm is essentially a reaction to Moore. Malcolm believes that common sense and
ordinary language are essentially the same thing, in
that to defend one is to defend the other. Malcolm
wonders if Moore is really defending common sense since
he violates ordinary language usage in his efforts to
do so. Malcolm claims that Moore is violating ordinary
language when he claims to <u>know</u> that he exists, has a
body, a consciousness, etc.. Perhaps a philosopher
might hold out his hand and entertain doubts about its
existence, but in ordinary everyday circumstances no
such doubt is possible. If doubt is impossible, then
knowledge claims are inappropriate. Hence, Malcolm concludes, to say "I know my hand exists" is to violate
ordinary language and hence common sense.

Woozley comes to Moore's defense by arguing that
ordinary language and common sense are quite different
things. Common sense has to do with beliefs, which can
be either expressed or unexpressed. The common sense
view of the world is a way of viewing the world. It is
not a view of how we use language. To violate ordinary
language is to violate the accepted criteria for correct
usage. To contradict a belief of common sense, on the
other hand, is to deny something which is either true or
false. Woozley's point is that Moore intended to be defending common sense beliefs, whether or not he violated
the rules of correct usage for ordinary language. As it
turns out, when common sense beliefs <u>are</u> expressed in
language they are almost always expressed in ordinary
language, so that appeal to ordinary usage may oft
times be quite useful. But, Woozley insists, to defend
common sense is to do much more than merely defend ordinary language usage.

A very different reaction to Moore's defense of common sense is presented in the selection entitled "Metaphysics and Common Sense" by A.J. Ayer. A.J. Ayer's name is generally associated with the philosophy of logical positivism and the attempted elimination of metaphysics. It is not surprising that in a discussion of metaphysics and common sense, Ayer favors the latter. But Ayer's attitude toward metaphysics is somewhat more sympathetic in this essay than one might expect. Ayer offers a fresh perspective on the relationship between metaphysics and common sense by showing that metaphysics has to do with external questions while common sense philosophy, such as Moore's, is really only concerned with internal questions. Internal questions are questions which arise within an established conceptual framework. They are settled by applying certain agreed upon criteria within that system. An external question is a question about the conceptual framework or system itself. Ayer suggests that by raising external questions, the metaphysician often provides a fresh way of looking at established conceptual schemes and frameworks. Ayer thinks that Moore's mistake was that of treating metaphysical questions as if they were internal rather than external questions. But within the conceptual framework of science and common sense Moore's victory is complete. If the metaphysician complains that the battle was fought on the wrong grounds, he is asking that we somehow get outside all conceptual systems, which Ayer says is impossible. Even our efforts to modify our intellectual outlook are doomed to failure if it does not at least roughly correspond to our ordinary way of looking at things. Echoing sentiments like those expressed by Rogers when he said that philosophy should be the handmaid of life, Ayer writes:

> ...if the philosopher is to succeed not merely in involving us in logical or semantic or epistemological puzzles but in altering or sharpening our vision of the world, he cannot leave common sense too far behind him.

Ayer does not believe that our thinking should be limited to the realm of common sense or the confines of ordinary language, but they do offer a curative to the sometimes wild speculations of the philosopher who has divorced himself from life. Still, Ayer concludes, "in philosophy, nothing should be absolutely sacrosanct: not even common sense."

The concluding essay on the value of philosophy begins with some reflections on the relationship between philosophy and our ordinary understanding of things. A pyramidic arrangement of our beliefs is suggested as a way of understanding the place of philosophical beliefs in relation to our other beliefs. Philosophy is viewed as the attempt to understand and evaluate our experience with, and beliefs about, the universe--at a level which ranges beyond the various sciences and arts. The central theme of this essay, and the general thesis of this entire collection of essays, is that philosophy divorced from our ordinary understanding of life is vain, and ordinary understanding unrefined by philosophical reflection is blind.

---

1. For a full account of Sidgwick's views on common sense, see my essay "Sidgwick's Common Sense Realism," Philosophy Research Archives, Vol. 13, No. 2, August, 1979.

2. Henry Sidgwick, The Methods of Ethics, 7th ed. (New York: Dover Publications, 1966), p. 373.

3. G.J. Warnock, English Philosophy Since 1900, 2nd ed. (New York: Oxford University Press, 1969), p. 13.

4. Paul Schilpp, ed., The Philosophy of G.E. Moore, (New York: Tudor Publishing Company, 1942), p. 16.

I. THE HANDMAID OF LIFE*

A. K. ROGERS

-taught philosophy at Yale University.

No man who is able to learn from experience at all, can live very long in the world without finding himself continually passing judgment, in one way or another, on the meaning and the value of life. At the very least there will be some things which it will seem to him to be worth the while to do, and other things, again, which will fail to interest him, and which by implication therefore he will condemn; but besides such fragmentary and instinctive judgments, he also, if he reflects at all, can hardly help but ask himself at times whether life has not some meaning as a whole, which would serve to throw light on the scattered and chaotic fragments of his everyday experience, and bring them into some degree of unity. Now philosophy, apart from technicalities of definition, is nothing but an attempt, in a reasoned and comprehensive way, to answer this question, What is the meaning of life? Everyone, therefore, in so far as he adopts a certain general attitude towards the problems that meet him, looks at them from a certain point of view, and does not simply let himself drift from one exper-

*From the Introduction to A Brief Introduction to Modern Philosophy (New York: The Macmillan Company, 1899).

ience to another without any purpose or unity to connect them, is taking the standpoint of philosophy. Such an attitude we call his philosophy of life, and if he is more or less clearly conscious of what this attitude is, and is able to express it in a unified and consistent way, we say in a popular sense that he is a philosopher. Technical philosophy differs from this only in the fact that it tries to do thoroughly, and in full consciousness of itself, what in popular thinking we do in a loose and unsystematic fashion. Instead of picking out those factors in life which appeal to us more personally and directly, it tries to set individual prejudices and limitations aside, and to include, as impartially as it can, all the elements which experience presents. It is true that in doing this it frequently gets far enough from what seem to be living interests; but back of all technical discussions, there is still the underlying conviction that by this path, and this alone, can we get at the vital and essential meaning of the world, or else we have no longer philosophy, but mere pedantry and hair-splitting. It is natural, then, that we should find the definitions which men have given of philosophy at different times are not by any means the same. They are not the same because, under different circumstances, men's interests are directed to different points, now to the importance of conduct, now to the nature of the external world, now to the existence of supersensible realities. But to say that their interest lies at one point or another, is only to say in other words that here they find the value of life; this is the test that can always be applied, the real motive, if not the apparent one. So we can speak of the philosophy of any pursuit whatever in which men can engage, or of any subject which can occupy them, of science, history and the philosophy of history, there is indeed no hard and fast separation; but what in the one case we are specially concerned with is the positive nature and the laws of a certain group of facts, which have been selected out from the rest of the world to be studied by themselves, while in the other we restore that connection with the whole which for the time being we had set aside, and try to look at our facts in the light of the meaning which they have for life in its entirety.

Even when it is stated in this preliminary way, the definition which has been given of philosophy will be seen to have a bearing on the disputes which have been common about the value of the study, and the very unequal estimation in which it has been held. There are many people to whom the pursuit of philosophy has seemed to be, at best, of very doubtful utility. Sometimes it is one who, like Matthew Arnold, is so impressed with the concrete values of art and conduct that the world of the philosopher seems to him abstract and barren in comparison. More often it is the man of science, who feels that he has got hold of reality so immediately and palpably in the world of matter, and of reality which is so far-reaching in its significance, that he has no interest left to give the supersensuous and very doubtful world which he understands that philosophy is trying to construct by merely thinking about it. Now the answer to be made to the scientist is this, that he is not getting along without philosophy, as he supposes, but only is adopting one particular kind of philosophy, whose implications, however, he does not try to understand. And he can hardly hold that this refusal to examine into the presuppositions of his thinking is, in opposition to the metaphysician's course, a highly meritorious thing, without stultifying his whole scientific procedure. He may, indeed, as a scientist, merely devote himself to the discovery of facts; but unless he is prepared to say that the bare objective fact is everything, and its meaning, its value for us, is nothing (which is very like a contradiction in terms), he cannot avoid encroaching on the philosopher's field. In reality he always does bring with him his own interpretation of the facts of science, and they differentiate the way in which he looks at the world from the way in which other men look at it; the only question is as to whether this should be conscious and thoroughgoing, or whether it should be unconscious, and unaware of the possible difficulties that may be involved. In any case the mere facts of the objective world, as objective, cannot exhaust the problems which arise, and arise necessarily, for this external world would not exist, for us, if it did not have a value as coming within our conscious life, and so it forms but a part of experience, not the whole. Whatever it may be in itself, for human interest at least the objective fact or law as such cannot possibly be a final and sufficient goal. Even the man who thinks that it is so, must have some reason why the search for objective truth appeals to him; its simple existence in itself does not explain why he should want to know it. It may of course be that, in the end, one might be driven to admit that no vital relation to human life could be discovered; in that case science at once would cease to be pursued. But answerable or not, at least it cannot be said that when the problems go beyond mere scientific matter of fact they cease to have any <u>interest</u> for us; knowing the chemical composition of water will not satisfy us in face of the larger question. What is this world of which our lives form a part? What is its meaning and destiny? And it is through philosophy, not through science, that this latter question must receive an answer, if it is answered at all.

Nevertheless there is some justification for this contemptuous attitude which science is apt to adopt towards philosophy, and which grows out of the true feeling that any value which is really worth our consideration must attach to the actual world in which we live, not to some far-away abstract world, which only can be got at by the occasional philosopher, and through the colorless medium of thought. What we are after is the meaning of life as we live it, and if we come out at the end with something that finds no place for the concrete values with which we are familiar, then certainly a large factor in the problem has without any justification been juggled out of sight. So that we have to insist, in the second place, that the data which the philosopher uses are not something which, by a pure act of intellectual creation, he spins out of his own head, but the same facts with which science, and history, and everyday living, deal. In this sense, therefore, the philosopher is dependent on the scientist; he cannot go his own way and construct his world <u>a</u> <u>priori</u>, but he must continually be falling back upon the concrete knowledge which science represents. So, also, philosophy does not "give us God, freedom, immortality," if by this we mean that it somehow puts us in possession of values which we had not before suspected. Religion, morality, the social life, all come before philosophy, and are presupposed by it;

and philosophy, in turn, in so far as it is only a bare recognition of truths, and not a vital appreciation of them, in so far as it stops with itself as mere knowing, and does not hand back the material which it has been elaborating intellectually, to the immediate experience in which this originated, is forgetting its place as the handmaid of life, and so is rendering itself barren and formal. All that philosophy can do is to take the actual values which come to us in experience, work out their implications and their mutual relationships, and, it may be, get at some unitary point of view, from which each element can be looked at, and have full justice done it. But by this very process it will be making a positive addition to the value of experience itself, not by creating truths which are entirely new, but by clearing up and throwing new light upon the meaning which already has been present in our lives, and so making it more real to us.

And this will also serve to indicate the answer to a very common complaint against philosophy, in which it is set over against feeling, as something quite opposed. It is common to hear people say, After all, it is feeling truth, not reasoning about it, which is the important thing; and philosophy, by translating everything over into the cold and impersonal medium of thought, and by introducing all sorts of doubts and limitations, is a foe to that immediate enjoyment of truth which alone is worth the having. Whether this is true or not depends entirely on what we mean by it. If we mean by feeling unintelligent, blind feeling, just the mere confused sense of satisfaction, it is not true at all. But this is not what we mean when we speak of feeling as it is aroused by poetry or art: that is equivalent rather to insight, intelligent appreciation. It is, therefore, not something which is opposed to reason, but its highest, most immediate exercise. But here again we shall be doing an injustice if we oppose immediacy too sharply to the more laborious and reflective work of thought. It is not philosophy which comes in to spoil the fineness of the enjoyment we get in immediate feeling, but it is the fact that feeling breaks down, and will no longer satisfy us, that compels us to betake ourselves to thought. Feelings are sure to clash, and then they possess no criterion within themselves which shall say whether this feeling or that one is the truer; merely as feeling they cannot tell us whether they are valid objectively, or whether we are only deluding ourselves with subjective emotions. To compare their values, and to bring them to the test of their consonancy with the whole of life, thought is needed; but that does not mean that we pass from immediate experience to something higher, thought; it means that, through thought, we get from an immediacy which is limited and partial, to one which is truer, richer, and more inclusive.

II.   THOUGHT AND TEMPERAMENT *

C. E. M. JOAD

   -former Scholar of Balliol College,
Oxford, and John Locke Scholar in Mental and
Moral Philosophy at Oxford University.

The question of the influence of temperament on thought, which is what I propose to discuss, appears to have first assumed importance in modern philosophy owing to the writings of William James.

   That such influence did exist, and that allowance must be made for it had always been recognised. There had always been a tendency, however, to rule it out of philosophical discussion, on the ground that pure thought as such was the only legitimate object of enquiry, and that in so far as thought was influenced by temperament it was to that extent not pure, and to that extent devoid of full significance. It is now, I think, generally recognised that thought and temperament, instinctive attitude, inherited tendency, call it what you will, are so inseparably intermingled that there is no such thing as an act of pure intellectual apprehension, just as there is no such thing as a desire entirely devoid of any intellectual element.

*This is the concluding essay in Joad's Essays in Common-Sense Philosophy, published in 1920, reissued in 1969 (Kennikat Press).

That a distinction does exist between them, namely, the common distinction that thought is universally the same, and that temperaments are individual and different, is assumed equally to be valid, and is an assumption which will be taken for granted in this essay.

Of all the divisions that have been made of the human race into two classes William James' is perhaps the most successful. It is in the main a mental one. He distinguishes two philosophic types, the "tender-minded" and the "tough-minded."

The "tender-minded" are "rationalistic, intellectualistic, idealistic, optimistic, religious, free-willist, monistic, and dogmatical."

The "tough-minded" are "empiricist, sensationalistic, materialistic, pessimistic, irreligious, fatalistic, pluralistic, sceptical." The gist of this distinction is, that the sort of creed you hold, the philosophic school you belong to, the view you take in purely intellectual matters, is to some extent conditioned by your character as a whole, and by your general outlook on life intellectual, emotional and instinctive. Certain types of view go with certain types of mind, and not only of mind but of character, and from your knowledge of the sort of man "A" is you can often predict fairly accurately the sort of opinions "A" will hold.

The fact that such a prediction can be made is of the greatest significance as regards the closeness of the relation between temperament and thought, and in particular, as indicating the influence of the first upon the second.

I hope to make the point clearer by some instances.

It is a well-known fact that nature exhibits both what is called design and lack of design. On the one hand we have multitudinous facts which lend support to the design theory. The maternal instinct is strongest when the offspring is weakest. Those flowers which can only be fertilised by the transference of the pollen from the male to the female flower are also most attractive to bees. Herodotus observed as a dual phenomenon that dangerous animals, such as the serpent, bring forth infrequently and with difficulty, but that the hare, which is preyed upon by all the other beasts, is defenceless, and provides adequate nourishment for the most varied tastes, has numerous offspring with the greatest facility. All these phenomena point to design in the plan of the Universe, and a Divine Intelligence planning and guiding the whole can be, and is, inferred from them.

A lack of design is, however, equally apparent if we look for it. A German writer, Lange, compared the workings of Nature to the actions of a man who, wishing to shoot a hare in a certain field, procured a thousand guns, surrounded the field, and caused them all to be shot off, or, desiring a house to live in, built a whole town, and abandoned to decay all the houses except one. Rain spoils the farmer's crops, and the mutual relations of animals to one another produce an impression of the grossest cruelty and injustice. From such phenomena it is a possible inference either that the Universe is entirely mindless, as Mr. Hardy sometimes appears to think, or that God, if there is one, is a malignant practical joker who created its anomalies solely for the amusement of contemplating them.

The interesting point is that where the tough-minded and the tender-minded man are presented with precisely the same phenomena as in the present instance, they will base opposite conclusions upon them, these conclusions being apparently dictated entirely by differences in the nature of the men who form them.

This result appears to be due to the different aspects of the phenomena under observation, to which different men will direct their attention according to their temperaments. Thus, while a devout Wesleyan will deduce from a still summer's evening of surpassing beauty evidence pointing to the power and goodness of God who created it, Mr. Hardy is primarily attracted by the "cry of some small bird that was being killed by an owl in the adjoining wood," from which the undrawn inference of the cruelty of the spirit, if any, behind nature is equally apparent.

To many minds the appearance of flowers in early

spring is an occasion for gladness, and a source of renewed hope in the signs of Nature's renewed life. Strindberg, however, finds his attention directed to other aspects of the same phenomenon. "Spring had come." he says, "the windows of the flower shops glowed with azaleas, and half-starved children were selling little bunches of liverworst in the street."

Thus the tender-minded man can find evidence for the beliefs to which his temperament predisposes him, just as the tough-minded man is furnished by the same material with matter for his contrary views. Temperament governs our attention. According to temperament we lay emphasis on different aspects of the same phenomena, and upon the aspects so selected our intellectual creed is founded. So that if temperament conditions selection, and selection intellectual conclusion, it may be asserted that in this respect at least thought is influenced by temperament.

If we now put the question, what was it that, abstracting all other irrelevant considerations as one might do in a novel, determined in the face of precisely the same scientific and critical data, whether a man would cleave to Agnosticism or Theosophy, the answer is his temperament. If tender-minded, he sided with Theosophy and belief, if tough with Agnosticism and doubt.

From a consideration of these and numerous other instances the following truth appears to emerge. Two men are faced with the same phenomena upon which conclusions are to be formed. The conclusions arrived at are often divergent and may be contradictory. All sorts of causes, such as those of environment, circumstance and upbringing may operate to effect the divergence, but it is often due largely, and sometimes wholly, to temperament alone.

If this conclusion be thought disturbing to our predilection that reason is, or should be free, the answer is that in most of its operations and over by far the largest fields of its activity, it is not free, and has not been considered so.

We are, for instance, confronted historically with

two main positions as to the function of reason in moral philosophy. Aristotle, who was tough-minded, and not sentimental about reason, held it to be the slave of the desires; Kant, who was presumably tender-minded, held that it dictated to them. For Aristotle desire both set the end of life and formulated the multitudinous individual ends which we pursue day by day. It was the business of reason acting subservient to this dictation to discover the steps by which these individual ends, and the end of life in general could be attained. For Kant, reason was free, and we only acted freely when obeying its dictates in opposition to those of passions; but Aristotle's has been perhaps the predominant tradition in moral philosophy, and with regard to most of the operations of reason there seems to be little doubt that Aristotle was right.

If reason acts mainly as the handmaid of desire we cannot say that we will think this or think that. What precisely we do think depends in a large degree upon our temperaments, the machinery of interaction being, as suggested above, the selection by reason according to our temperaments of different aspects of a given whole as the material upon which reason forms her conclusions.

The fact that our convictions, formed as many of them are in virtue of our temperaments, are not matters of free will, is the root justification of toleration, and freedom from persecution in religious matters. For our religious convictions are in a pre-eminent degree dependent upon temperament, belief being a highly composite affair, including many elements besides the purely rational, and as a rule requiring some quality of enthusiasm as an ingredient which is associated less frequently with scepticism. A fanatical or persecuting Agnostic, though a possible phenomenon, is a rare one.

The case of mysticism sets forth the matter in the plainest light. It is, I think, generally recognised that mysticism pre-supposes a peculiar kind of temperament rather than a peculiar set of intellectual convictions. The mystic, like the ascetic, is always thought of as being such and such a man, rather than as holding such and such beliefs. Mysticism involves a certain attitude towards things which are not capable of being either explained or understood. The matters with which mysticism is concerned cannot be either explained or understood simply because mysticism, if it could give an account of itself, would cease to be mysticism. But whereas the tender-minded will regard such matters as being above understanding, and therefore sacred, the tough-minded will regard them as being unfit for understanding, and therefore valueless. The tender-minded reveres what is beyond him, the tough denies it.

The tough-minded man calls everything to the bar of intelligence, and if it can give no account of itself condemns it. He regards mysticism, Theosophy and all doctrines which make more demands upon a man's faith than upon his intelligence, as the resource of secondrate minds, which have been driven to shelter themselves behind bulwarks of dogma, as a protection from the assaults of their intellectual superiors in the open field. Finding that intellect is not their forte they cry "These grapes are sour," disclaim its sovereignty, and affirm that the most essential truths about life, God, immortality, and the nature of the Universe cannot be grasped by intellect at all. If this is the attitude of the tough-minded with regard to the Shibboleths of the tender-minded, the latter takes his revenge by pointing to the chaos of belief achieved by philosophy, and is almost inclined to say that the more you trust to intellect the further you drift from truth. For such a mind mysticism is the only salvation from the barren quibbles of logic, which by enabling you to prove everything, turns round in your hands, and ends in proving nothing; for the tough-minded it is God's last ditch, the barrier erected by the intellectually unfit to save their self-respect from the defeats administered to orthodox religion by Evolution and the Higher Criticism.

The same divergence can be distinguished in the fundamental positions taken up by philosophers with regard to the ultimate constitution of the Universe and the significance of human consciousness upon it, positions which form the basis of clear cut intellectual creeds, such as those of Monism and Pluralism, but which are originally embraced from temperamental reasons.

William James speaks specifically of the clash between what he calls the cynical and the sympathetic temper, from which materialistic and spiritualistic philosophies are the rival types that result. The former defines the world, and feels no spiritual pang of loneliness at so defining it, as something in essence alien to human consciousness, which appears upon it purely as an incidental phenomenon, "a sort of outside passenger" without unique significance or participation in the real essence of the Universe. The world contains many different things, and human consciousness is just one of them, a mere eddy in the primaeval slime, hence Pluralism. The latter "insists that the intimate and human must surround and underlie the brutal." The nature of reality must be something akin to human consciousness, from which it is but a step to say that all human consciousnesses are part of one another and of it, hence Monism.

* * *

These two fundamental attitudes are not so much a matter of intellectual conviction as of general mental make-up, a make-up not devoid of emotional and temperamental elements. The spiritual attitude regards a Universe alien in structure, as intolerably lonely and hostile, and tends to endow it with something of its own nature for solace and, as it were, for spiritual company. The materialistic consciousness is not overwhelmed at the thought of its own insignificance in an alien world, stands bravely alone, makes much of its hardihood in facing unpalatable facts, and regards it as no intellectual gain to falsify them for the purpose of gaining emotional consolation. Thus William James regards the Absolute with its sense of all embracing intimacy, as a "large seaside boarding house with no private bedroom in which I might take refuge from the society of the place." It appears in fact that James did not logically convince himself on intellectual grounds that the doctrine of the Absolute was wrong, and then suddenly evolve these feelings of emotional antipathy to it. The antipathy was fundamental and original, and influenced his thought in the direction of finding intellectual reasons to justify it. It is not too much to say that the divergences of all our conclusions may be at bottom conditioned by the different selections of facts on which they are based, and though it may be arguable whether, were we all presented with

the same factual data without power of selection from
them, we should all hold the same views, there would
be at least much more unanimity than there is under
present conditions.

   Our convictions, then, are formed by the intellect
but they are formed upon emotional bases. It is matter
for conjecture and ultimately for decision on temperamental grounds whether this enhances or invalidates
their truth. M. Sabatier has written a book purporting
to prove the existence of God. The religious sentiment
is shown therein to be fundamental and is traced through
its evolutionary stages from witchcraft and devil wor-
ship to the refined and elaborate product of to-day.
Most significant, he thinks, is the additional strength
of the religious impulse, the craving for sympathy and
the passionate desire to turn to an interested and personal God in times of trouble and distress. When our
confidence in ourselves is least our confidence in God
is greatest. Thus on purely emotional and sentimental
phenomena is based on intellectual conviction that a
personal God exists, the fact that our belief is grounded in the emotion being held to add to its value and
enhance its validity. God must be there, it is thought,
or we should not all feel so strongly that He is there.
The Agnostic will feel inclined to doubt this reasoning.
Our emotional states may dictate our beliefs, he will
say, but that does not prove them true. Belief in God
is irrational, <u>because</u> it is founded on emotion. At
most we can have a reasonable expectation that the assumption of a deity is the most probable explanation of
certain material and psychological phenomena. The mere
fact, he would say, that you are led to your belief by
the emotional comfort it affords should make you sus-
picious of its validity. Such a belief is open to the
same kind of suspicion as that which attaches to the
smoker's cherished conviction that tobacco ash is good
for the carpet.

   Once again the tough dissents from the tendermind-
ed in his interpretation of the same phenomena, the
phenomena about which they differ being in this case
concerned with the very matter of which we are treating, namely, the significance of thought which is
influenced and dictated by emotion. Whereas the tender-
minded man considers on the whole that the value of such

thought is enhanced, the tough holds that it is diminished. Unpalatable truths, he would maintain, are valuable, not so much because they are true, but because they are unpalatable; yet even so they are far more likely to be true than palatable ones, for we tend to believe unpalatable truths because they are true, and palatable ones because they are pleasant.

*   *   *

It is conceivable that, reason as such being uniform, the deliverances of unbiassed reason upon identical phenomena would also be uniform; this, of course, presuming we could confine reason in a watertight compartment and regard its action as isolated. The existence of controversy and differences of opinion would then be sufficiently accounted for merely by the influence of temperamental and emotional factors upon it. In the last satire of Gulliver, Swift gives us a picture of equine perfection and unanimity which is guided by reason alone, i.e., reason unwarped by temperament.

"Neither is reason among them," he says, speaking of the Houyhnhnms, "a point problematical as among us where men can argue with plausibility on both sides of a question, but strikes you with immediate conviction, as it must needs do where it is not mingled, obscured, or discovered by passion and interest. I remember that it was with extreme difficulty that I could bring my master to understand the meaning of the word 'opinion,' or how a point could be disputable, because reason taught us to affirm or deny only where we are certain, and beyond our knowledge we cannot do either."

This leads us to a consideration of that branch of knowledge and that kind of reasoning which appears to be mainly, if not wholly, exempt from the influence of temperament.

It would appear that in the forefront of such knowledge we must place mathematical truths. The conviction that the proposition two plus two makes four is true is an intellectual conviction, and apparently unanimously subscribed to by people of every kind of temperament. All purely mathematical truths appear to be of this kind deriving the unanimity with which they are embraced from the fact that it is not possible for the human mind to conceive them to be otherwise. The apprehension of most scientific truths which are formed by generalisation upon a number of instances, such as the law of gravitation, also appears to come under this category. The same holds true of certain moral truths, i.e., those that are concerned with classes of actions. Although there is the greatest divergence as to the rightness or wrongness of actions in particular instances, as for example whether one ought to tell this particular lie in these particular circumstances, a question which may very frequently be decided in accordance with temperamental considerations, the tough-minded man tending to decide by utilitarian criteria and the tender to insist on following what he calls his intuitions, and to ignore the consequences, we all agree to condemn lying generally wrong.

It may well be that all the occupations which may or have been ascribed to an omnipotent mind are exempt from temperamental influences. Thus Aristotle regards mathematics as pre-eminently the object of contemplation of the deity, who is, according to his view, non-temperamental, and mathematics does seem to be pre-eminently the study, excellence or stupidity in which can be ascribed exclusively to excellence or deficiency in the reasoning faculty, and not to the warping or stimulating influence of any form of temperament whatsoever, excepting always the existence of that curiosity which is fundamentally at the root of any intellectual pursuit, and which even a mathematician cannot afford to be without.

Much controversy exists, as we have seen, both as to the nature and number of the Platonic ideas. While, however, Plato's belief in the Forms of hair and mud is a matter of dispute, there are certain ideas as to the existence of which there can no doubt be maintained continuous and unswerving allegiance. On reduction and exclusion of all doubtful cases these appear to be the idea of Truth, the idea of Beauty, and the idea of Goodness. There was always something peculiar about these ideas such that the transcendentalising of them does not appear to be nonsense, but, granting their existence, a not improbable fact. It may of course be coincidence, but these ideas appear to be set over against just those activities of the mind which have seemed to us to be exempt from temperamental influence. We may differ, as pointed out above, in the degree of our appreciation of sunsets, but there is no recorded instance of a civilised man who did not think sunsets beautiful.

This peculiarity of our mental attitudes towards the ideas of truth, beauty and goodness is usually expressed by saying that these concepts are not purely subjective. Something objective exists in these cases, of which appreciation may be full or meagre, but in so far as we are human beings at all we cannot fail to appreciate it in some degree, however minute. And this appreciation though the precise form it takes may be conditioned by our temperament, is not dependent for its existence upon it. Our appreciation of sunsets may be ecstatic or it may be tranquil; that depends upon whether we are excitable or placid people; but the existence of the appreciation of obvious beauty, just like the existence of the apprehension of obvious mathematical truth, appears to be unconditioned by temperamental considerations.

Can the same be said of philosophical thought? It would seem not. Our philosophical views appear to be distinguished from our mathematical knowledge, in that the former are views and open to dispute, while the latter is knowledge and not controverted. This distinction is mainly due to the difference between the objects studied.

The objects studied by mathematicians are in a sense abstractions. The integer two is arrived at originally by an abstraction from instances, e.g., two men, two ponies, two pineapples. In mathematics, however, we are occupied with The Two. In Philosophy we are concerned with The Two, and with the two men, the two ponies and the two pineapples, and the relations between them. We are concerned, in fact with everything, we contemplate life itself.

Now our attitude to life in general is a different thing from our intellectual apprehension of the functions and powers of certain unchangeable realities. Our attitude to life in general embraces all our faculties, and includes among other things that intellectual contemplation of our attitude to life which is the main subject of this chapter. Unlimited possibilities of infinite regress here present themselves. Just as the most disturbing thing about being worried about yourself is the fact that you get worried about being worried about yourself, you realise in fact that you have nerves, so the mere fact of recognising that you possess an attitude towards life leads to speculation about that recognition, a speculation which is bound to some extent to be modified in its conclusions according to the nature of the attitude it studies. The experiences of an ascetic hermit are plainly different from those of a prosperous merchant. Contemplation by each of his experiences must necessarily lead to different views as to the aims of life and the object and nature of the Universe. The ascetic, contemplating his experience, concludes that the appetites are unimportant but that the control of them is important. The business man, in so far as he contemplates himself at all, tends on the whole to arrive at the opposite conclusion. The Universe can, in fact, only be interpreted through the medium of our own experience of it; our experiences are largely conditioned by our temperaments, which have led us to choose them, and our intellectual creed, which is leavened by the material of experience upon which it is formed, indirectly reflects the temperament which is responsible for the material.

* * *

If any degree of truth can be claimed for the foregoing arguments, if it is really true that what we think is largely conditioned by what we feel, if our views of truth, rightness and justice are frequently and largely dependent upon inborn peculiarities of temperament, the case for toleration, always strong, is tremendously strengthened. We can say we will do this or we will do that, remarks Mr. Shaw, but we cannot say that we will like doing this or like doing that, that in fact, we will feel like this or feel like that. If then our feelings are beyond our control, so to a large extent are our views. Consequently we should extend the widest toleration to apparently wrong-headed people who disagree with us, on the ground that they are not responsible for their apparent wrongheadedness. They are not responsible, not on deterministic but on temperamental grounds. We shall not say, it was fated he should think so and so, but he is the sort of man who necessarily would think so and so.

It may be that every man's temperament naturally fits him for such and such a one particularly, of all the intellectual beliefs of his age (or at any rate of some age), so that if we could imagine all the various attitudes to every controversial question of the day, moral, political, religious and scientific, every question upon which, if a man thinks at all he must necessarily take up some attitude, exhibited for inspection as it were at a sale, practically every man would find one, at least, to fit his temperament like a glove. Those who do not are geniuses who think in advance of their time and consequently unpopular. They create opinions instead of adopting them.

Hence the enormous importance of allowing every child and man access to every kind of literature, that he may find at last that view of life to which his own temperament predisposes him, and may thereafter specialise in his special intellectual department. And finally that is why persecution and intolerance, unwise and unjust upon any view, take on a fresh aspect of evil on this and become irrational also.

All persecution, it is not too much to say all propaganda, arises from the curious inability of the human mind to think anything by itself. Directly we hold a belief to be true we desire to communicate it to others, directly we think such and such things desirable we endeavour to make others think them desirable also. The inventor who has discovered a new method of cookery immediately bruits abroad his opinion that to cook in his way and no other is rational, and does not rest until he has persuaded others to agree with his opinion. The fanatic who thinks that God should be worshipped in one particular way and one only, is ready to roast or excommunicate whoever does not think likewise. The State Socialist who believes that maternity should be endowed continually publishes tracts with the object of making others share his opinion. If men originally desire originality it is only in order that their own originality may become universalised into orthodoxy. No man wishes to be original all by himself. It may be that this tendency arises from a sort of spiritual loneliness of the kind attributed to tender-minded philosophers above, which leads them to endow the Universe with a something not alien to their own consciousness. Just as man appears to be social politically he appears to be social mentally. No philosopher is really content with the conviction that he has found truth. He is lonely with truth and is not content until others share it. Hence propaganda, and, in extreme cases, persecution. But once grant that our selection of truth is not free, but that our choice is conditioned in part by temperament, and the irrationality of endeavouring to make others see truth as we see it becomes overwhelmingly clear.

III. PRAGMATISM AND COMMON
             SENSE*

William James

    -taught philosophy and psychology at
    Harvard University. He is recognized as one
    of the leading figures in the school of
    American Pragmatism.

In respect of the knowledge it contains the world does
genuinely change and grow. Some general remarks on
the way in which our knowledge completes itself - when
it does complete itself - will lead us very conveniently
into our subject for this lecture, which is 'Common
Sense.'

    To begin with, our knowledge grows in spots. The
spots may be large or small, but the knowledge never
grows all over: some old knowledge always remains what
it was. Your knowledge of pragmatism, let us suppose,
is growing now. Later, its growth may involve considerable modification of opinions which you previously
held to be true. But such modifications are apt to be

*From Pragmatism (1907), reissued by David McKay Com-
pany, New York, Reprinted with permission of the publishers.

gradual. To take the nearest possible example, consider these lectures of mine. What you first gain from them is probably a small amount of new information, a few new definitions, or distinctions, or points of view. But while these special ideas are being added, the rest of your knowledge stands still, and only gradually will you 'line up' your previous opinions with the novelties I am trying to instill, and modify to some slight degree their mass.

You listen to me now, I suppose, with certain prepossessions as to my competency, and these affect your reception of what I say, but were I suddenly to break off lecturing, and to begin to sing 'We won't go home till morning' in a rich baritone voice, not only would that new fact be added to your stock, but it would oblige you to define me differently, and that might alter your opinion of the pragmatic philosophy, and in general bring about a rearrangement of a number of your ideas. Your mind in such processes is strained, and sometimes painfully so, between its older beliefs and the novelties which experience brings along.

Our minds thus grow in spots; and like grease-spots, the spots spread. But we let them spread as little as possible: we keep unaltered as much of our old knowledge, as many of our old prejudices and beliefs, as we can. We patch and tinker more than we renew. The novelty soaks in; it stains the ancient mass; but it is also tinged by what absorbs it. Our past apperceives and co-operates; and in the new equilibrium in which each step forward in the process of learning terminates, it happens relatively seldom that the new fact is added raw. More usually it is embedded cooked, as one might say, or stewed down in the sauce of the old.

New truths thus are resultants of new experiences and of old truths combined and mutually modifying one another. And since this is the case in the changes of opinion of today, there is no reason to assume that it has not been so at all times. It follows that very ancient modes of thought may have survived through all the later changes in men's opinions. The most primitive ways of thinking may not yet be wholly expunged. Like our five fingers, our ear-bones, our rudimentary caudal appendage, or our other 'vestigial' peculiarities, they may remain as indelible tokens of events in our race-history. Our ancestors may at certain moments have struck into ways of thinking which they might conceivably not have found. But once they did so, and after the fact, the inheritance continues. When you begin a piece of music in a certain key, you must keep the key to the end. You may alter your house ad libitum, but the ground-plan of the first architect persists - you can make great changes, but you can not change a Gothic church into a Doric temple. You may rinse and rinse the bottle, but you can't get the taste of the medicine or whiskey that first filled it wholly out.

My thesis now is this, that our fundamental ways of thinking about things are discoveries of exceedingly remote ancestors, which have been able to preserve themselves throughout the experience of all subsequent time. They form one great stage of equilibrium in the human mind's development, the stage of common sense. Other stages have grafted themselves upon this stage, but have never succeeded in displacing it. Let us consider this common-sense stage first, as if it might be final.

In practical talk, a man's common sense means his good judgment, his freedom from excentricity, his gumption, to use the vernacular word. In philosophy it means something entirely different, it means his use of certain intellectual forms or categories of thought. Were we lobsters, or bees, it might be that our organization would have led to our using quite different modes from these of apprehending our experiences. It might be too (we can not dogmatically deny this) that such categories, unimaginable by us to-day, would have proved on the whole as serviceable for handling our experiences mentally as those which we actually use.

If this sounds paradoxical to any one, let him think of analytical geometry. The identical figures which Euclid defined by intrinsic relations were defined by Descartes by the relations of their points to adventitious co-ordinates, the result being an absolutely different and vastly more potent way of handling curves. All our conceptions are what the Germans call Denkmittel, means by which we handle facts by thinking them. Experience merely as such doesn't come ticketed and labelled, we have first to discover what it is.

Kant speaks of it as being in its first intention a
gewuhl der erscheinungen, a rhapsodie der wahrnehm-
ungen, a mere motley which we have to unify by our wits.
What we usually do is first to frame some system of
concepts mentally classified, serialized, or connected
in some intellectual way, and then to use this as a
tally by which we 'keep tab' on the impressions that
present themselves. When each is referred to some possible place in the conceptual system, it is thereby
'understood.' This notion of parallel 'manifolds' with
their elements standing reciprocally in 'one-to-one relations,' is proving so convenient nowadays in mathematics and logic as to supersede more and more the older
classificatory conceptions. There are many conceptual
systems of this sort; and the sense manifold is also
such a system. Find a one-to-one relation for your
sense-impressions anywhere among the concepts, and in
so far forth you rationalize the impressions. But obviously you can rationalize them by using various conceptual systems.

The old common-sense way of rationalizing them is
by a set of concepts of which the most important are
these:
Thing;
The same or different;
Kinds;
Minds;
Bodies;
One Time;
One Space;
Subjects and attributes;
Causal influences;
The fancied;
The real.

We are now so familiar with the order that these
notions have woven for us out of the everlasting weather of our perceptions that we find it hard to realize
how little of a fixed routine the perceptions follow
when taken by themselves. The word weather is a good
one to use here. In Boston, for example, the weather
has almost no routine, the only law being that if you
have had any weather for two days, you will probably
but not certainly have another weather on the third.
Weather-experience as it thus comes to Boston is dis-

continuous, and chaotic. In point of temperature, of wind, rain or sunshine, it may change three times a day. But the Washington weather-bureau intellectualizes this disorder by making each successive bit of Boston weather episodic. It refers it to its place and moment in a continental cyclone, on the history of which the local changes everywhere are strung as beads are strung upon a cord.

Now it seems almost certain that young children and the inferior animals take all their experiences very much as uninstructed Bostonians take their weather. They know no more of time, or space, as world-receptacles, or of permanent subjects and changing predicates, or of causes, or kinds, or thoughts, or things, than our common people know of continental cyclones. A baby's rattle drops out of his hand, but the baby looks not for it. It has 'gone out' for him, as a candle-flame goes out; and it comes back, when you replace it in his hand, as the flame comes back when relit. The idea of its being a 'thing,' whose permanent existence by itself he might interpolate between its successive apparitions has evidently not occurred to him. It is the same with dogs. Out of sight, out of mind, with them. It is pretty evident that they have no general tendency to interpolate 'things.' Let me quote here a passage from my colleague G. Santayana's book.
"If a dog, while sniffing about contentedly, sees his master arriving after a long absence...the poor brute asks for no reason why his master went, why he has come again, why he should be loved, or why presently while lying at his feet you forget him and begin to grunt and dream of the chase - all that is an utter mystery, utterly unconsidered. Such experience has variety, scenery, and a certain vital rhythm; its story might be told in dithyrambic verse. It moves wholly by inspiration; every event is providential, every act unpremeditated. Absolute freedom and absolute helplessness have met together: you depend wholly on divine favor, yet that unfathomable agency is not distinguishable from your own life.
...(But) the figures even of that disordered drama have their exits and their entrances; and their cues can be gradually discovered by a being capable of fixing his attention and retaining the order of events....In proportion as such understanding advances, each moment of

experience becomes consequential and prophetic of the rest. The calm places in life are filled with power and its spasms with resource. No emotion can overwhelm the mind, for of none is the basis or issue wholly hidden; no event can disconcert it altogether, because it sees beyond. Means can be looked for to escape from the worst predicament; and whereas each moment had been formerly filled with nothing but its own adventures and surprised emotion, each now makes room for the lesson of what went before and surmises what may be the plot of the whole."[1]

Even to-day science and philosophy are still laboriously trying to part fancies from realities in our experience; and in primitive times they made only the most incipient distinctions in this line. Men believed whatever they thought with any liveliness, and they mixed their dreams with their realities inextricably. The categories of 'thought' and 'things' are indispensable here - instead of being realities we now call certain experiences only 'thoughts.' There is not a category, among those enumerated, of which we may not imagine the use to have thus originated historically and only gradually spread.

That one Time which we all believe in and in which each event has its definite date, that one Space in which each thing has its position, these abstract notions unify the world incomparably; but in their finished shape as concepts how different they are from the loose unordered time-and-space experiences of natural men! Everything that happens to us brings its own duration and extension, and both are vaguely surrounded by a marginal 'more' that runs into the duration and extension of the next thing that comes. But we soon lose all our definite bearings; and not only do our children make no distinction between yesterday and the day before yesterday, the whole past being churned up together, but we adults still do so whenever the times are large. It is the same with spaces. On a map I can distinctly see the relation of London, Constantinople, and Pekin to the place where I am; in reality I utterly fail to <u>feel</u> the facts which the map symbolizes. The directions and distances are vague, confused and mixed. Cosmic space and cosmic time, so far from being the intuitions that Kant said they were, are constructions as patently artificial as any that science can show. The great majority of the human race never use these notions, but live in plural times and spaces, interpenetrant and durcheinander.

Permanent 'things' again; the 'same' thing and its various 'appearances' and 'alterations'; the different 'kinds' of thing; with the 'kind' used finally as a 'predicate,' of which the thing remains the 'subject' - what a straightening of the tangle of our experience's immediate flux and sensible variety does this list of terms suggest! And it is only the smallest part of his experience's flux that any one actually does straighten out by applying to it these conceptual instruments. Out of them all our lowest ancestors probably used only, and then most vaguely and inaccurately, the notion of 'the same again.' But even then if you had asked them whether the same were a 'thing' that had endured throughout the unseen interval, they would probably have been at a loss, and would have said that they had never asked that question, or considered matters in that light.

Kinds, and sameness of kind - what colossally useful denkmittel for finding our way among the many! The manyness might conceivably have been absolute. Experiences might have all been singulars, no one of them occurring twice. In such a world logic would have had no application; for kind and sameness of kind are logic's only instruments. Once we know that whatever is of a kind is also of that kind's kind, we can travel through the universe as if with seven-league boots. Brutes surely never use these abstractions, and civilized men use them in most various amounts.

Causal influence, again! This, if anything, seems to have been an antediluvian conception; for we find primitive men thinking that almost everything is significant and can exert influence of some sort. The search for the more definite influences seems to have started in the question: "Who, or what, is to blame?" - for any illness, namely, or disaster, or untoward thing. From this centre the search for causal influences has spread. Hume and 'Science' together have tried to eliminate the whole notion of influence, substituting the entirely different denkmittel of 'law.' But law is a comparatively recent invention, and influence reigns supreme in the older realm of common sense.

The 'possible,' as something less than the actual and more than the wholly unreal, is another of these magisterial notions of common sense. Criticise them as you may, they persist; and we fly back to them the moment critical pressure is relaxed. 'Self,' 'body,' in the substantial or metaphysical sense - no one escapes subjection to <u>those</u> forms of thought. In practice, the common-sense <u>denkmittel</u> are uniformly victorious. Every one, however instructed, still thinks of a 'thing' in the common-sense way, as a permanent unit-subject that 'supports' its attributes interchangeably. No one stably or sincerely uses the more critical notion, of a group of sense-qualities united by a law. With these categories in our hand, we make our plans and plot together, and connect all the remoter parts of experience with what lies before our eyes. Our later and more critical philosophies are mere fads and fancies compared with this natural mother-tongue of thought.

Common sense appears thus as a perfectly definite stage in our understanding of things, a stage that satisfies in an extraordinarily successful way the purposes for which we think. 'Things' do exist, even when we do not see them. Their 'kinds' also exist. These lamps shed their quality of light on every object in this room. We intercept <u>it</u> on its way whenever we hold up an opaque screen. It is the very sound that my lips emit that travels into your ears. It is the sensible heat of the fire that migrates into the water in which we boil an egg; and we can change the heat into coolness by dropping in a lump of ice. At this stage of philosophy all non-European men without exception have remained. It suffices for all the necessary practical ends of life; and, among our race even, it is only the highly sophisticated specimens, the minds debauched by learning, as Berkeley calls them, who have ever even suspected common sense of not being absolutely true.

But when we look back, and speculate as to how the common-sense categories may have achieved their wonderful supremacy, no reason appears why it may not have been by a process just like that by which the conceptions due to Democritus, Berkeley, or Darwin, achieved their similar triumphs in more recent times. In other words, they may have been successfully <u>discovered</u> by prehistoric geniuses whose names the <u>night of</u> antiquity has covered up; they may have been verified by the immediate facts of experience which they first fitted; and then from fact to fact and from man to man they may have <u>spread</u>, until all language rested on them and we are now incapable of thinking naturally in any other terms. Such a view would only follow the rule that has proved elsewhere so fertile, of assuming the vast and remote to conform to the laws of formation that we can observe at work in the small and near.

For all utilitarian practical purposes these conceptions amply suffice; but that they began at special points of discovery and only gradually spread from one thing to another, seems proved by the exceedingly dubious limits of their application to-day. We assume for certain purposes on 'objective' Time that <u>aequabiliter fluit</u>, but we don't livingly believe in or <u>realize</u> any such equally-flowing time. 'Space' is a less vague notion; but 'things,' what are they? Is a constellation properly a thing? or an army? or is an <u>ens rationis</u> such as space or justice a thing? Is a knife whose handle and blade are changed the 'same'? Is the 'changeling,' whom Locke so seriously discusses, of the human 'kind'? Is 'telepathy' a 'fancy' or a 'fact'? The moment you pass beyond the practical use of these categories (a use usually suggested sufficiently by the circumstances of the special case) to a merely curious or speculative way of thinking, you find it impossible to say within just what limits of fact any one of them shall apply.

The peripatetic philosophy, obeying rationalist propensities, has tried to eternalize the common-sense categories by treating them very technically and articulately. A 'thing' for instance is a being, or <u>ens</u>. An <u>ens</u> is a substance. Substances are of kinds, and <u>kinds</u> are definite in number, and discrete. These distinctions are fundamental and eternal. As terms of <u>discourse</u> they are indeed magnificently useful, but what they mean, apart from their use in steering our discourse to profitable issues, does not appear. If you ask a scholastic philosopher what a substance may be in itself, apart from its being the support of attributes, he simply says that your intellect knows perfectly what the word means.

But what the intellect knows clearly is only the word itself and its steering function. So it comes about that intellects sibi permissi, intellects only curious and idle, have forsaken the common-sense level for what in general terms may be called the 'critical' level of thought. Not merely such intellects either-- you Humes and Berkeleys and Hegels; but practical observers of facts, you Galileos, Daltons, Faradays, have found it impossible to treat the naive sense-termini of common sense as ultimately real. As common sense interpolates her constant 'things' between our intermittent sensations, so science extrapolates her world of 'primary' qualities, her atoms, her ether, her magnetic fields, and the like, beyond the common-sense world. The 'things' are now invisible impalpable things; and the old visible common-sense things are supposed to result from the mixture of these invisibles. Or else the whole naive conception of thing gets superseded, and a thing's name is interpreted as denoting only the law or regal der verbindung by which certain of our sensations habitually succeed or coexist.

Science and critical philosophy thus burst the bounds of common sense. With science naive realism ceases: 'Secondary' qualities become unreal; primary ones alone remain. With critical philosophy, havoc is made of everything. The common-sense categories one and all cease to represent anything in the way of being; they are but sublime tricks of human thought, our ways of escaping bewilderment in the midst of sensation's irremediable flow.

But the scientific tendency in critical thought, though inspired at first by purely intellectual motives, has opened an entirely unexpected range of practical utilities to our astonished view. Galileo gave us accurate clocks and accurate artillery-practice; the chemists flood us with new medicines and dye-stuffs; Ampere and Faraday have endowed us with the New York subway and with Marconi telegrams. The hypothetical things that such men have invented, defined as they have defined them, are showing an extraordinary fertility in consequences verifiable by sense. Our logic can deduce from them a consequence due under certain conditions, we can then bring about the conditions, and presto, the consequence is there before our eyes. The scope of the practical control of nature newly put into our hand by scientific ways of thinking vastly exceeds the scope of the old control grounded on common sense. Its rate of increase accelerates so that no one can trace the limit; one may even fear that the being of man may be crushed by his own powers, that his fixed nature as an organism may not prove adequate to stand the strain of the ever increasingly tremendous functions, almost divine creative functions, which his intellect will more and more enable him to wield. He may drown in his wealth like a child in a bath-tub, who has turned on the water and who can not turn it off.

The philosophic stage of criticism, much more thorough in its negations than the scientific stage, so far gives us no new range of practical power. Locke, Hume, Berkeley, Kant, Hegel, have all been utterly sterile, so far as shedding any light on the details of nature goes, and I can think of no invention or discovery that can be directly traced to anything in their peculiar thought, for neither with Berkeley's tarwater nor with Kant's nebular hypothesis had their respective philosophic tenets anything to do. The satisfactions they yield to their disciples are intellectual, not practical; and even then we have to confess that there is a large minus-side to the account.

There are thus at least three well-characterized levels, stages or types of thought about the world we live in, and the notions of one stage have one kind of merit, those of another stage another kind. It is impossible, however, to say that any stage as yet in sight is absolutely more true than any other. Common sense is the more consolidated stage, because it got its innings first, and made all language into its ally. Whether it or science be the more august stage may be left to private judgment. But neither consolidation nor augustness are decisive marks of truth. If common sense were true, why should science have had to brand the secondary qualities, to which our world owes all its living interest, as false, and to invent an invisible world of points and curves, and mathematical equations instead? Why should it have needed to transform causes and activities into laws of 'functional variation'? Vainly did scholasticism, common sense's college-trained younger sister, seek to stereotype the forms the human family had always talked with, to make them definite and fix them for eternity. Substantial forms (in other words our secondary qualities) hardly outlasted the year of our Lord 1600. People were already tired of them then; and Galileo, and Descartes, with his 'new philosophy,' gave them only a little later their coup de grace.

But now if the new kinds of scientific 'thing,' the corpuscular and etheric world, were essentially more 'true,' why should they have excited so much criticism within the body of science itself? Scientific logicians are saying on every hand that these entities and their determinations, however definitely conceived, should not be held for literally real. It is as if they existed; but in reality they are like co-ordinates or logarithms, only artificial short-cuts for taking us from one part to another of experience's flux. We can cipher fruitfully with them; they serve us wonderfully; but we must not be their dupes.

There is no ringing conclusion possible when we compare these types of thinking, with a view to telling which is the more absolutely true. Their naturalness, their intellectual economy, their fruitfulness for practice, all start up as distinct tests of their veracity, and as a result we get confused. Common sense is better for one sphere of life, science for another, philosophic criticism for a third; but whether either be truer absolutely, Heaven only knows. Just now, if I understand the matter rightly, we are witnessing a curious reversion to the common sense way of looking at physical nature, in the philosophy of science favored by such men as Mach, Ostwald and Duhem. According to these teachers no hypothesis is truer than any other in the sense of being a more literal copy of reality. They are all but ways of talking on our part, to be compared solely from the point of view of their use. The only literally true thing is reality; and the only reality we know is, for these logicians, sensible reality, the flux of our sensations and emotions as they pass. 'Energy' is the collective name (according to Ostwald) for the sensations just as they present themselves (the movement, heat, magnetic pull, or light, or whatever it may be) when they are measured in certain ways. So measuring them, we are enabled to describe the correlated changes which they show us, in formulas matchless for their simplicity and fruitfulness for human use. They are sovereign triumphs of economy in thought.

No one can fail to admire the 'energetic' philosophy. But the hypersensible entities, the corpuscles and vibrations, hold their own with most physicists and chemists, in spite of its appeal. It seems too economical to be all-sufficient. Profusion, not economy, may after all be reality's key-note.

I am dealing here with highly technical matters, hardly suitable for popular lecturing, and in which my own competence is small. All the better for my conclusion, however, which at this point is this. The whole notion of truth, which naturally and without reflexion we assume to mean the simple duplication by the mind of a ready-made and given reality, proves hard to understand clearly. There is no simple test available for adjudicating offhand between the divers types of thought that claim to possess it. Common sense, common science or corpuscular philosophy, ultra-critical science, or energetics, and critical or idealistic philosophy, all seem insufficiently true in some regard and leave some dissatisfaction. It is evident that the conflict of these so widely differing systems obliges us to overhaul the very idea of truth, for at present we have no definite notion of what the word may mean.

There are only two points that I wish you to retain from the present lecture. The first one relates to common sense. We have seen reason to suspect it, to suspect that in spite of their being so venerable, of their being so universally used and built into the very structure of language, its categories may after all be only a collection of extraordinarily successful hypotheses (historically discovered or invented by single men, but gradually communicated, and used by everybody) by which our forefathers have from time immemorial unified and straightened the discontinuity of their immediate experiences, and put themselves into an equilibrium with the surface of nature so satisfactory for ordinary practical purposes that it certainly would have lasted forever, but for the excessive intellectual vivacity of Democritus, Archimedes, Galileo, Berkeley, and of other excentric geniuses whom the example of such men inflamed. Retain, I pray you, this suspicion about common sense.

The other point is this. Ought not the existence of the various types of thinking which we have reviewed, each so splendid for certain purposes, yet all conflicting still, and neither one of them able to support a claim of absolute veracity, to awaken a presumption favorable to the pragmatistic view that all our theories are <u>instrumental</u>, are mental modes of <u>adaptation</u> to reality, rather than revelations or gnostic answers to some divinely instituted world-enigma?

---

1. <u>The Life of Reason: Reason in Common Sense</u>, 1905, p. 59.

IV. WHAT IS COMMON SENSE?*

THOMAS REID

-was Professor of Moral Philosophy at
Glasgow and founded of the Scottish School
of Common Sense Realism.

Meaning of the Term Common Sense. This inward light or
sense is given by Heaven to different persons in different degrees. There is a certain degree of it which
is necessary to our being subjects of law and government, capable of managing our own affairs, and answerable for our conduct towards others: this is called
common sense, because it is common to all men whom we
can transact business with, or call to account for their
conduct.

The laws of all civilized nations distinguish those
who have this gift of Heaven from those who have it not.
The last may have rights which ought not to be violated,
but, having no understanding in themselves to direct
their actions, the laws appoint them to be guided by the
understanding of others. It is easily discerned by its
effects in men's actions, in their speeches, and even in
their looks; and when it is made a question, whether a

*From Essays on the Intellectual Powers of Man, Chapter
II, Essay VI (Cambridge: M.I.T. Press, 1969). Reprinted
with permission of the publishers.

man has this natural gift or not, a judge or a jury, upon a short conversation with him, can, for the most part, determine the question with great assurance.

The same degree of understanding which makes a man capable of acting with common prudence in the conduct of life, makes him capable of discovering what is true and what is false in matters that are self-evident, and which he distinctly apprehends. All knowledge, and all science, must be built upon principles that are self-evident; and of such principles, every man who has common sense is a competent judge, when he conceives them distinctly. Hence it is, that disputes very often terminate in an appeal to common sense. While the parties agree in the first principles on which their arguments are grounded, there is room for reasoning; but when one denies what to the other appears too evident to need or to admit of proof, reasoning seems to be at an end; an appeal is made to common sense, and each party is left to enjoy his own opinion.

There seems to be no remedy for this, nor any way left to discuss such appeals, unless the decisions of common sense can be brought into a code, in which all reasonable men shall acquiesce. This, indeed, if it were possible, would be very desirable, and would supply a desideratum in logic; and why should it be thought impossible that reasonable men should agree in things that are self-evident?

All that is intended in this chapter is to explain the meaning of common sense, that it may not be treated, as it has been by some, as a new principle, or as a word without any meaning. I have endeavoured to show, that sense, in its most common, and therefore its most proper meaning, signifies judgment, though philosophers often use it in another meaning. From this it is natural to think, that common sense should mean common judgment; and so it really does.

What the precise limits are which divide common judgment from what is beyond it, on the other, may be difficult to determine; and men may agree in the meaning of the word who have different opinions about those limits, or who even never thought of fixing them. This is as intelligible as that all Englishmen should mean

the same thing by the county of York, though perhaps
not a hundredth part of them can point out its precise
limits. Indeed, it seems to me that common sense is as
unambiguous a word, and as well understood, as the
county of York. We find it in innumerable places in
good writers; we hear it on innumerable occasions in
conversation; and, as far as I am able to judge, always
in the same meaning. And this is probably the reason
why it is so seldom defined or explained.

* * *

Dr. Johnson, in the authorities he gives to show
that the word sense signifies understanding, soundness
of faculties, strength of natural reason, quotes Dr.
Bentley for what may be called a definition of common
sense, though probably not intended for that purpose,
but mentioned accidentally: - "God hath endowed mankind
with power and abilities, which we call natural light
and reason, and common sense."

* * *

Men rarely ask what common sense is; because every
man believes himself possessed of it, and would take it
for an imputation upon his understanding to be thought
unacquainted with it.

* * *

I apprehend that whatever censure is thrown upon
those who have spoken of common sense as a principle of
knowledge, or who have appealed to it in matters that
are self-evident, will fall light, when there are so
many to share in it. Indeed, the authority of this tribunal is too sacred and venerable, and has prescription
too long in its favor, to be now wisely called in question. Those who are disposed to do so may remember the
shrewd saying of Mr. Hobbes, - "When reason is against a
man, a man will be against reason." This is equally applicable to common sense.

Relation of Reason and Common Sense to each other.
It is absurd to conceive that there can be any opposition between reason and common sense. It is, indeed,
the first-born of reason, and, as they are commonly

joined together in speech and in writing, they are inseparable in their nature.

We ascribe to reason two offices, or two degrees. The first is to judge of things self-evident; the second to draw conclusions that are not self-evident from those that are. The first of these is the province, and the sole province, of common sense; and therefore, it coincides with reason in its whole extent, and is only another name for <u>one branch or one degree of reason</u>. Perhaps it may be said, Why, then, should you give it a particular name, since it is acknowledged to be only a degree of reason? It would be a sufficient answer to this, Why do you abolish a name which is to be found in the language of all civilized nations, and has acquired a right by prescription? Such an attempt is equally foolish and ineffectual. Every wise man will be apt to think, that a name which is found in all languages as far back as we can trace them, is not without some use.

But there is an obvious reason why this degree of reason should have a name appropriated to it; and that is, that <u>in the greatest part of mankind no other degree of reason is to be found</u>. It is this degree that entitles them to the denomination of reasonable creatures. It is this degree of reason, and this only, that makes a man capable of managing his own affairs, and answerable for his conduct towards others. There is, therefore, the best reason why it should have a name appropriated to it.

These two degrees of reason differ in other respects, which would be sufficient to entitle them to <u>distinct</u> names.

The first is purely <u>the gift of Heaven</u>. And where Heaven has not given it, no education can supply the want. The second is <u>learned by practice and rules</u>, when the first is not wanting. A man who has common sense may be taught to reason. But if he has not that gift, no teaching will make him able either to judge of first principles or to reason from them.

I have only this further to observe, that the province of common sense is <u>more extensive in refutation</u>

than in confirmation. A conclusion drawn by a train of just reasoning from true principles cannot possibly contradict any decision of common sense, because truth will always be consistent with itself. Neither can such a conclusion receive any confirmation from common sense, because it is not within its jurisdiction.

But it is possible, that, by setting out from false principles, or by an error in reasoning, a man may be led to a conclusion that contradicts the decisions of common sense. In this case, the conclusion is within the jurisdiction of common sense, though the reasoning on which it was grounded be not; and a man of common sense may fairly reject the conclusion, without being able to show the error of the reasoning that led to it. Thus, if a mathematician, by a process of intricate demonstration, in which some false step was made, should be brought to this conclusion, that two quantities, which are equal to a third, are not equal to each other, a man of common sense, without pretending to be a judge of the demonstration, is well entitled to reject the conclusion, and to pronounce it absurd.

V. THE PHILOSOPHY OF COMMON
             SENSE*

HENRY SIDGWICK

   -was Knightbridge Professor of Moral
   Philosophy at Cambridge University.

   I propose to present to you such features of Reid's
philosophical work as appear to me of most enduring
interest.

   The appeal to vulgar common sense has an important
place in Reid's doctrine: he does rely on it: nor can I
defend him from the charge that he relies on it too much.
He does hold that the mere ridiculousness of Hume's conclusions is a good reason for disbelieving them: and
even in his later and maturer treatise he speaks of the
sense of the ridiculous as a guide to philosophic truth,
in language that lacks his usual circumspection. For
our sense of the ridiculous is manifestly stirred by the
mere incongruity of an opinion with our intellectual habits: a strange truth is no less apt to excite it than a
strange error. When the Copernican theory was slowly
winning its way to acceptance, even the grave Milton al-

*From The Philosophy of Kant and Other Lectures (1905),
reissued by Kraus Reprint Company (1968). Reprinted
with permission of the publishers.

lowed himself a jest on "the new carmen who drive the earth about": and I can remember how, when the Darwinian theory was new, persons of the highest culture cracked their jokes on the zoologist's supposed private reasons for the absurd conclusion that his ancestor was a monkey. And this is doubtless all for the best: laughter is a natural and valuable relief in many perplexities and disturbances of life, and I do not see why it should not relieve the disturbance caused by the collision of new opinions with old: only let us remember that it is evidence of nothing except the mere fact of collision. But, though Reid does rely more than he ought on the <u>argumentum ad risum</u>, he is not so stupid as to think that a volume is required to exhibit this argument. He does say to the plain man, "If philosophy befools her votaries, and leads them into these quagmires of absurdity, beware of her as an <u>ignis fatuus</u>": but he immediately adds, "Is it, however, certain that this fair lady is of the party? Is it not possible that she may have been misrepresented?" and that she has been misrepresented is the thesis which he aims at proving.

In the course of the proof, no doubt, he leads us again to Common Sense, as the source and warrant of certain primary data of knowledge at once unreasoned and indubitable: but the Common Sense to which we are thus led is not that of the vulgar as contrasted with the philosopher: Reid's point is that the philosopher inevitably shares it with the vulgar. Whether a philosopher has been developed out of a monkey may possibly be still an open question; but there can be no doubt that he is developed out of a man; and if we consider his intellectual life as a whole, we may surmise that the larger part of it is occupied with the beliefs that he still shares with the unphilosophical majority of his contemporaries. It is on this fact that Reid's appeal to him is based. He refers to Hume's account of the manner in which, after solitary reflection has environed him with the clouds and darkness of doubt, the genial influence of "dinner, backgammon, and social talk" dispels these doubts and restores his belief in the world without and the self within: and Reid takes his stand with those who are "so weak as to imagine that they ought to have the same belief in solitude and in company." His <u>essential</u> demand, therefore, on the philosopher, is not <u>primarily</u> that he should make his beliefs

50

consistent with those of the vulgar, but that he should
make them consistent with his own; and the legitimacy
of the demand becomes, I think, more apparent, when we
regard it as made in the name of Philosophy rather than
in the name of Common Sense. For when we reflect on
plain Common Sense, - on the body of unreasoned principles of judgment which we and other men are in the ha-
bit of applying in ordinary thought and discourse, - we
find it certainly to some extent confused and inconsistent: but it is not clear that it is the business of
Common Sense to get rid of these confusions and inconsistencies, so long as they do not give trouble in the
ordinary conduct of life: at any rate it is not its most
pressing business, since system-making is not its affair.
But system-making is pre-eminently the affair of Philosophy, and it cannot willingly tolerate inconsistencies:
at least if it has to tolerate them, as I sadly fear
that it has, it can only tolerate them as a physician
tolerates a chronic imperfection of health, which he can
only hope to mitigate and not completely to cure.

Accordingly, in Reid's view it is the duty of a
philosopher--his duty _as_ a philosopher--to aim steadily
and persistently at bringing the common human element of
his intellectual life into clear consistency with the
special philosophic element. And Reid is on the whole
perfectly aware--though his language occasionally ig-
nores it--that for every part of this task the special
training and intellectual habits of the philosopher are
required. For the fundamental beliefs which the philosopher shares with the plain man can only be defined with
clearness and precision by one who has reflected system-
atically, as an ordinary man does not reflect, on the
operations of his own mind; even the elementary distinction between sensation and perception is, Reid admits,
only apprehended by the plain man in a confused form.
To bring the distinction into clear consciousness, to
attend to "sensation and perception each by itself, and
to attribute nothing to one which belongs to the other,"
requires, he tells us, "a degree of attention to what
passes in our own minds, and a talent for distinguishing
things that differ, which is not to be expected in the
vulgar." The philosopher alone can do it: but in order
to do it, he must partially divest himself of his philosophic peculiarities; that is, he must temporarily put
out of his mind the conclusions of any system he may

have learnt or adopted, and merely bring his trained faculty of reflective attention to the observation and analysis of the common human element of his thought.

But if it be admitted that the philosopher alone is capable of the steady and clear attention required to ascertain the fundamental beliefs of Common Sense, what valid evidence is there of the general assent to these beliefs on which Reid lays stress, and which, indeed, the term implies? He seems to be in a dilemma; either the many must be held capable of reflective analysis, or the decision on questions of fundamental belief must after all be limited to the expert few. The difficulty is partly met by pointing out that the philosophical faculty required to distinguish and state such beliefs with precision much exceeds that required to judge of such a statement when made; just as few of us could have found out the axioms required in the study of geometry, but we could easily see the truth of Euclid's at a very early age. Still, granting this, I think that Reid presses too far the competence of plain men even to judge of philosophical first principles. It is true, as he urges, that this judgment requires no more than a "sound mind free from prejudice and a distinct conception of the questions": but it does not follow, as Reid seems to think, that "every man is a competent judge, the learned and unlearned, the philosopher and day-labourer alike": because a good deal of the painful process we call 'learning' is normally needed to realise these apparently simple requirements, freedom from prejudice and distinctness of conception. I will not affirm that no day-labourer could attain a distinct conception of the positions that Reid is defending against Berkeley and Hume: but I venture to think that a day-labourer who could convince us that he had attained it would be at once recognised as a born philosopher, incontrovertibly qualified by native genius for membership of the society that I have the honour to address.

At the same time, I cannot think Reid wrong in holding that the propositions he is most concerned to maintain as first principles are implicitly assented to by men in general. That for ordinary men sense-perception involves a belief in the existence of a thing perceived, independent of the perception: that similarly consciousness involves a belief in the existence of a permanent identical subject of changing conscious states: that ordinary moral judgment involves the belief in a real right and wrong in human action, capable of being known by a moral agent and distinct in idea from what conduces to his interest: that in ordinary thought about experience we find implicit the unreasoned assumption that every change must have a cause, and a cause adequate to the effect,--all this, I think, will hardly be denied by any one who approaches the question with a fair mind. He may, of course, still regard it as unphilosophical to rest the validity of these beliefs on the fact of their general acceptance. But here again it must be said that Reid's own deference to general assent is of a strictly limited and subordinate kind. He is far from wishing truth to be determined by votes: he only urges that "authority, though tyrannical as a mistress, is useful as a handmaid to private judgment." He points out that even in the exactest sciences authority actually has this place: even a mathematician who has demonstrated a novel conclusion is strengthened in his belief in it by the assent of other mathematical experts who have examined his demonstration, and is "reduced to a kind of suspense" by their dissent.

    This is, I think, undeniable: and perhaps we may separate Reid's just and moderate statement of the claims of Authority from his exaggerated view of the competence of untrained intellects to deal with philosophical first principles; and simply take it as a cardinal point in the philosophy of Common Sense that a difference in judgment from another whom he has no reason to regard as less competent to judge than himself, naturally and properly reduces a thinker to a "kind of suspense." When the conflict relates to a demonstrated conclusion, it leads him to search for a flaw in the opponent's demonstration; but when it relates to a first principle, primary datum, or fundamental assumption, this resource appears to be excluded: and then, perhaps, when he has done all that he can to remove any misunderstanding of the question at issue, the Common Sense philosopher may be allowed to derive some support from the thought that his own conviction is shared by the great majority of those whose judgments have built up and continually sustain the living fabric of our common thought and knowledge.

And this, I think, is all that Reid really means to claim.

I have now, I hope, succeeded in making clear the general relation which Reid's epistemology bears to his psychology. I have not used these modern terms, because Reid himself blends the two subjects under the single notion of "Philosophy of the Human Mind": but it is necessary, in any careful estimate of his work, to distinguish the process of psychological distinction and analysis through which the fundamental beliefs of Common Sense are ascertained, from the arguments by which their validity is justified. I do not propose to enter into the details of Reid's psychological view, which has largely become antiquated through the progress of mental science. But if Locke is the first founder of the distinctively British study, Empirical Psychology, of which the primary method is introspective observation and analysis, I think Reid has a fair claim to be regarded as a second founder: and even now his psychological work may be studied with interest, from the patient fidelity of his self-observation, the acumen of his reflective analysis, and especially, his entire freedom from the vague materialism that, in spite of Descartes, still hung about the current philosophical conception of Mind and its operations. It is, indeed, in the task of exposing the unwarrantable assumptions generated by this vague materialism that the force and penetration of Reid's intellect is most conspicuously shown.

Let me briefly note this in the case of the beliefs involved in ordinary sense-perception, since this problem occupies a leading place in his discussion. Not, I ought to say, that he is specially interested in this problem on its own account: he makes it quite clear that it is on far greater issues that his thought is really set. God, Freedom, Duty, the spirituality of human nature,--these are, for Reid as for Kant, the grave matters really at stake in the epistemological controversy. But these greater matters, for the very reason of their supreme importance, are apt to stir our deepest emotions so strongly as to render difficult the passionless precision of analysis and reasoning which Reid rightly held to be needful for the attainment of philosophical truth: while at the same time it is clear to him that all the questions hang together, and that the decision of one in the sense that he claims will carry with it the similar determination of the rest.

Accepting this view then, and remembering that in a trivial case we are trying no trivial issue, let us examine his treatment of the cognition by Mind of particular material things. Here Reid's task, as he ultimately saw, was merely carrying further the work of Descartes. By clearly distinguishing the motions of material particles antecedent to perception from perception itself as a psychical fact, Descartes had got rid of the old psychophysical muddle, by which forms or semblances of things perceived by the senses were supposed somehow to get into the brain through the 'animal spirits' and so into the mind. But he had not equally got rid of the view that perception was the getting of an idea in the mind, from which the existence of a thing outside the mind <u>like</u> the idea had to be somehow inferred. This view is definitely held, not only by his disciple Malebranche but by his independent successor Locke. They do not see what Reid came to see, that the normal perception of an external object presents itself to introspection as an immediate cognition: that is, as a cognition which has no psychical mediation, no inference in it. What prevented them and others from seeing this was, mainly, a naive assumption that the mind can only know immediately what is 'present' to it, and that things outside the body cannot be thus present; as the mind cannot go out to them and they cannot get into the mind, only the ideas of them can get in. It was reserved to Reid to point out the illegitimacy of this assumption, and to derive it from a confused, half-unconscious transfer to Mind and its function of cognition, of the conditions under which body acts on body in ordinary physical experience. When the assumption is made explicit and traced to its source, it loses, I think, all appearance of validity.

It is to be observed, that in affirming external perception to be an immediate cognition, Reid does not of course mean that it is physically uncaused. He only means that the perceiving mind has not a double object, its own percept and a non-mental thing like its percept: and accordingly that our normal conviction of the present existence of the non-mental thing perceived is not a judgment attained by reasoning, but a primary datum of knowledge. He recognises like his predecessors that it has physical antecedents, movements of material particles both without and within the organism. And he recognises, more distinctly than his predecessors, that it has psychical antecedents and concomitants, i.e. sensations which he carefully distinguishes from the perception that they suggest and accompany. A consideration of these antecedents may possibly affect our reflective confidence in the cognition that follows them,--that question I will deal with presently,--but at any rate it cannot properly modify our view of the content of this cognition as ascertained by introspective observation. This, I think, remains true after duly taking account of the valuable work that has been done since Reid's time, in ascertaining more accurately the antecednets and concomitants of our common perceptions of extended matter. Whatever view we may take on the interesting but still disputed questions as to the precise manner in which visual, tactual, and muscular feelings have historically been combined in the genesis of our particular perceptions and general notions of matter and space,--there can still be no doubt of the fundamental difference in our present consciousness between these perceptions or notions and any combinations of muscular, tactual, and visual feelings.

It has indeed been held, by an influential school of British psychologists, that this manifest difference is merely apparent and illusory: it has been held that by a process of "mental chemistry" sensations and images of sensation have been "compounded" into what we now distinguish as perceptions and conceptions of matter in space, and that the latter really consist of sensations and images of sensation, just as water really consists of oxygen and hydrogen. But this view involves a second illegitimate transfer of physical conditions to psychical facts; and Reid would certainly have rejected 'mental chemistry' in this application as unhesitatingly as he does reject it when applied to support the conclusion that a "cluster of the ideas of sense, properly combined, may make up the idea of a mind." He would have rejected it for the simple reason that we have no ground for holding any fact of consciousness to be other than careful introspection declares it to be. In the case of material chemistry, the inference that a compound consists of certain elements depends on experimental proof that we can not only make the compound out of the elements, but can also make the elements again out of the compound. But even if we grant that our cognitions of Matter and Space, of Self and Duty, are derived from more elementary feelings, it is certain that no psychical experiment will enable us to turn them into such feelings again: the later phenomena, if products, are biological not chemical products, resulting from evolution, not from mere composition.

Still, it may be said, granting the existence of cognitions and beliefs that cannot now be resolved into more elementary feelings, and that present themselves in ordinary thought with the character of unreasoned certitude, systematic reflection on these beliefs and their antecedents must render it impossible to accept them as trustworthy premises for philosophical reasoning. It is a commonplace that the senses deceive, and the more we learn of the psychophysical process of sense-perception, the more clear it becomes why and how they must deceive. Even apart from cases of admitted illusion, philosophical reflection on normal perception continually shows us, as Hume urges, a manifest difference between the actual percept and what we commonly regard as the real thing perceived. Thus, Hume says, "the table which we see seems to diminish as we remove farther from it: but the real table which exists independent of us suffers no alteration. It was, therefore, nothing but its image which was present to the mind. These are the obvious dictates of reason." In answering this line of objection Reid partly relies on a weak distinction between original and acquired perception, which the progress of science has rendered clearly untenable and irrelevant. Apart from this his really effective reply is twofold. First he points out that the very evidence relied upon to show the unreality of sense-percepts really affords striking testimony to the general validity of the belief in an independent reality known through sense-perception. It is by trusting, not by distrusting, this fundamental belief that Common Sense organised into Science continually at once corrects and confirms crude Common Sense. Take Hume's case of the table. If nothing but images were present to the mind, how could we ever know that there exists a real table which does not alter while the visible magnitude changes with its distance from us? The plain man knows this through an acquired perception, by which he habitually judges of real magnitude from visible appearances: but science carries the knowledge further, enabling us to predict exactly what appearance a given portion of extended matter will exhibit at any given distance from the spectators. Now all this coherent, precise, and unerring prediction rests upon innumerable sense-perceptions; and the scientific processes which have made it possible have been carried on throughout on the basis of the vulgar belief in the independent existence of the matter perceived. "Is it not absurd," Reid asks, "to suppose that a false supposition of the vulgar has been so lucky in solving an infinite number of phenomena of nature?"

Suppose, however, that the opponent resists this argument: suppose he maintains that, though physical science may find the independent existence of matter a convenient fiction,--as mathematicians find it convenient to feign that they can extract the square root of negative quantities,--still in truth Mind can only know mental facts--feelings and thoughts. Suppose he further urges that the common belief in the independent existence of the object of perception is found on reflection to have no claim to philosophic acceptance, because while admittedly unreasoned it cannot be said to be strictly intuitive:--granted that I may directly perceive that it exists independently of my perception. To this line of argument Reid has another line of reply. He points out to the Idealist that he does not escape from this kind of unreasoned belief by refusing to recognise a reality beyond consciousness. He has still to rely on data of knowledge which are open to the same objections as the belief in the independent existence of matter. For instance, he has to rely on memory. If sense-perception is fallible, memory is surely more fallible; if we do not know intuitively and cannot prove that what we perceive really exists independently of our perception, still less can we either know intuitively or prove that what we recollect really happened: if on reflection we find it difficult to conceive how the Non-ego can be known by the Ego, there is surely an equal difficulty in understanding how the present Ego can know the Past. And yet once cease to rely on memory, and intellectual life becomes impossible: even in reasoning beyond the very simplest we have to rely on our recollection of previous steps of reasoning. A pure system of truths reasoned throughout from rational intuitions may be the philosophic ideal: but it is as true of the intellectual as of the physical life that living somehow is prior to living ideally well: and if we are to live at all, we must accept some beliefs that cannot claim Reason for their source. Is it not then, Reid urges, arbitrary and unphilosophical to acquiesce tranquilly in some of these beliefs of Common Sense, and yet obstinately to fight against others that have an equal warrant of spontaneous certitude? May we not rather say that it is the duty of a philosopher to give impartially a provisional acceptance to all such beliefs, and then set himself to clarity them by reflection, remove inadvertencies, confusions, and contradictions, and as far as possible build together the purged results into an ordered and harmonious system of thought?

If, finally, the opposing philosopher answers that he cannot be satisfied by any system that is not perfectly transparent to reason, Reid does not altogether refuse him his sympathy, though he cannot encourage him to hope. "I confess," he says, "after all that the evidence of reasoning, and of necessary and self-evident truths, seems to be the least mysterious and the most perfectly comprehended. . . the light of truth so fills my mind in these cases that I can neither conceive nor desire anything more satisfying. On the other hand, when I remember distinctly a past event, or see an object before my eyes," though "this commands my belief no less than an axiom. . . I seem to want that evidence which I can best comprehend and which gives perfect satisfaction to an inquisitive mind." And "to a philosopher who has been accustomed to think that the treasure of his knowledge is the acquisition of his reason, it is no doubt humiliating to find" that "his knowledge of what really exists or did exist comes by another channel," and that "he is led to it" as it were "in the dark." "It is no wonder" then "that some philosophers should invent vain theories to account for this knowledge": while others "spurn at a knowledge they cannot account for and vainly attempt to throw it off." But all such "attempts," he holds, are as impracticable as "an attempt to fly."

The passage from which I have quoted was published in 1785, when Reid was seventy-five years of age. Even before it was published attempts at aerial navigation had suddenly come to seem less chimerical in the physical world ; and before the end of the century, in the world of thought, attempts to transcend and rationally account for the beliefs of Common Sense--more remarkable than any dreamt of by Reid--had begun to excite some interest even in our insular mind. The nineteenth century is now drawing to its close; and these attempts to fly are still going on, both in the physical and in the intellectual world; but in neither region, according to my information, have they yet attained a triumphant success. At the same time our age, which has seen so many things achieved that were once thought impossible, may without presumption contemplate such attempts in a somewhat more hopeful spirit than was possible to Reid: and I should be sorry to say anything here to damp the noble ardour or to depress the high aspirations that ought to animate a society like yours. But if there should be any one among you who, desirous to philosophise and yet fearing the fate of Icarus, may prefer to walk in the dimness and twilight of the lower region in which my discourse has moved,--then I venture to think that he may even now find profit in communing with the earnest, patient, lucid, and discerning intellect of the thinker who, in the history of modern speculation, has connected the name of Scotland with the Philosophy of Common Sense.

VI.   A   DEFENCE   OF   COMMON

                  SENSE*

       GEORGE EDWARD MOORE

          -former Professor of Philosophy and Fellow
       of Trinity College in the University of Cam-
       bridge.

   In what follows I have merely tried to state, one by
one, some of the most important points in which my
philosophical position differs from positions which
have been taken up by some other philosophers. It may
be that the points which I have had room to mention are
not really the most important, and possibly some of
them may be points as to which no philosopher has ever
really differed from me. But, to the best of my belief,
each is a point as to which many have really differed;
although (in most cases, at all events) each is also a
point as to which many have agreed with me.

       I. The first point is a point which embraces a

*The exerpts in this chapter are from "A Defence of
Common Sense" in Philosophical Papers and "What is Philosophy?" in Some Main Problems in Philosophy (London:
George Allen & Unwin, Publishers). Reprinted with permission of the publishers.

                        61

great many other points. And it is one which I cannot state as clearly as I wish to state it, except at some length. The method I am going to use for stating it is this. I am going to begin by enunciating, under the heading (1), a whole long list of propositions, which may seem, at first sight, such obvious truisms as not to be worth stating: they are, in fact, a set of propositions, every one of which (in my own opinion) I _know_, with certainty, to be true. I shall, next, under the heading (2), state a single proposition which makes an assertion about a whole set of _classes_ of propositions --each class being defined, as the class consisting of all propositions which resemble _one_ of the propositions in (1) in a certain respect. (2), therefore, is a proposition which could not be stated, until the list of propositions in (1), or some similar list, had already been given. (2) is itself a proposition which may seem such an obvious truism as not to be worth stating: and it is also a proposition which (in my own opinion) I _know_, with certainty, to be true. But, nevertheless, it is, to the best of my belief, a proposition with regard to which many philosophers have, for different reasons, differed from me; even if they have not directly denied (2) itself, they have held view incompatible with it. My first point, then, may be said to be that (2), together with all its implications, some of which I shall expressly mention, is true.

(1) I begin, then, with my list of truisms, every one of which (in my own opinion) I _know_, with certainty, to be true. The propositions to be included in this list are the following:

There exists at present a living human body, which is _my_ body. This body was born at a certain time in the past, and has existed continuously ever since, though not without undergoing changes; it was, for instance, much smaller when it was born, and for some time afterwards, than it is now. Ever since it was born, it has been either in contact with or not far from the surface of the earth; and, at every moment since it was born, there have also existed many other things, having shape and size in three dimensions (in the same familiar sense in which it has), from which it has been at _various distances_ (in the familiar sense in which it is now at a distance both from that mantelpiece and from that bookcase, and at a greater distance from the bookcase than it is from the mantelpiece); also there have (very often, at all events) existed some other things of this kind with which it was in <u>contact</u> (in the familiar sense in which it is now in contact with the pen I am holding in my right hand and with some of the clothes I am wearing). Among the things which have, in this sense, formed part of its environment (i.e. have been either in contact with it, or at <u>some</u> distance from it, however <u>great</u>) there have, at every moment since its birth, been large numbers of other living human bodies, each of which has, like it, (a) at some time been born, (b) continued to exist from some time after birth, (c) been, at every moment of its life after birth, either in contact with or not far from the surface of the earth; and many of these bodies have already died and ceased to exist. But the earth had existed also for many years before my body was born; and for many of these years, also, large numbers of human bodies had, at every moment, been alive upon it; and many of these bodies had died and ceased to exist before it was born. Finally (to come to a different class of propositions), I am a human being, and I have, at different times since my body was born, had many different experiences, of each of many different kinds: e.g. I have often perceived both my own body and other things which formed part of its environment, including other human bodies; I have not only perceived things of this kind, but have also observed facts about them, such as, for instance, the fact which I am now observing, that that mantelpiece is at present nearer to my body than that bookcase; I have been aware of other facts, which I was not at the time observing, such as, for instance, the fact, of which I am now aware, that my body existed yesterday and was then also for some time nearer to that mantelpiece than to that bookcase; I have had expectations with regard to the future, and many beliefs of other kinds, both true and false; I have thought of imaginary things and persons and incidents, in the reality of which I did not believe; I have had dreams; and I have had feelings of many different kinds. And, just as my body has been the body of a human being, namely myself, who has, during his lifetime, had many experiences of each of these (and other) different kinds; so, in the case of very many of the other human bodies which have lived upon the earth, each has been the body of a different human being, who has, during the lifetime of that body, had many different experiences of each of these (and other) different kinds.

(2) I now come to the single truism which, as will be seen, could not be stated except by reference to the whole list of truisms, just given in (1). This truism also (in my own opinion) I know, with certainty, to be true; and it is as follows:

In the case of very many (I do not say all) of the human beings belonging to the class (which includes myself) defined in the following way, i.e. as human beings who have had human bodies, that were born and lived for some time upon the earth, and who have, during the lifetime of those bodies, had many different experiences of each of the kinds mentioned in (1), it is true that each has frequently, during the life of his body, known, with regard to himself or his body, and with regard to some time earlier than any of the times at which I wrote down the propositions in (1), a proposition corresponding to each of the propositions in (1), in the sense that it asserts with regard to himself or his body and the earlier time in question (namely, in each case, the time at which he knew it), just what the corresponding proposition in (1) asserts with regard to me or my body and the time at which I wrote that proposition down.

In other words what (2) asserts is only (what seems an obvious enough truism) that each of us (meaning by 'us', very many human beings of the class defined) has frequently known, with regard to himself or his body and the time at which he knew it, everything which, in writing down my list of propositions in (1), I was claiming to know about myself or my body and the time at which I wrote that proposition down, i.e. just as I knew (when I wrote it down) 'There exists at present a living human body which is my body', so each of us has frequently known with regard to himself and some other time the different but corresponding proposition, which he could then have properly expressed by, 'There exists at present a human body which is my body'; just as I know 'Many human bodies other than mine have before now lived on the earth', so each of us has frequently known the different but corresponding proposition 'Many human bodies other than mine have before now lived on the earth';

just as <u>I</u> know 'Many human beings other than myself have before now perceived, and dreamed, and felt', so each of <u>us</u> has frequently known the different but corresponding proposition 'Many human beings other than <u>myself</u> have before <u>now</u> perceived, and dreamed, and felt'; and so on, in the case of <u>each</u> of the propositions enumerated in (1).

I hope there is no difficulty in understanding, so far, what this proposition (2) asserts. I have tried to make clear by examples what I mean by 'propositions <u>corresponding</u> to each of the propositions in (1)'. And what (2) asserts is merely that each of us has frequently known to be true a proposition <u>corresponding</u> (in that sense) to each of the propositions in (1)--a <u>different</u> corresponding proposition, of course, at each of the times at which he knew such a proposition to be true.

*　　*　　*

If this first point in my philosophical position, namely my belief in (2), is to be given any name, which has actually been used by philosophers in classifying the positions of other philosophers, it would have, I think, to be expressed by saying that I am one of those philosophers who have held that the 'Common Sense view of the world' is, in certain fundamental features, <u>wholly</u> true. But it must be remembered that, according to me, <u>all</u> philosophers, without exception, have agreed with me in holding this: and that the real difference, which is commonly expressed in this way, is only a difference between those philosophers, who have <u>also</u> held views inconsistent with these features in 'the Common Sense view of the world', and those who have not.

The features in question (namely, propositions of any of the classes defined in defining (2)) are all of them features, which have this peculiar property--namely, that <u>if we know that they are features in the 'Common Sense view of the world', it follows that they are true</u>: it is self-contradictory to maintain that we know them to be features in the Common Sense view, and that yet they are not true; since to say that <u>we</u> know this, is to say that they are true. And many of them also have the further peculiar property that, <u>if they are</u>

features in the Common Sense view of the world (whether 'we' know this or not), it follows that they are true, since to say that there is a 'Common Sense view of the world' or 'Common Sense beliefs' (as used by philosophers) are, of course, extraordinarily vague; and, for all I know, there may be many propositions which may be properly called features in 'the Common Sense view of the world' or 'Common Sense beliefs', which are not true, and which deserve to be mentioned with the contempt with which some philosophers speak of 'Common Sense beliefs'. But to speak with contempt of those 'Common Sense beliefs' which I have mentioned is quite certainly the height of absurdity. And there are, of course, enormous numbers of other features in 'the Common Sense view of the world' which, if these are true, are quite certainly true too: e.g. that there have lived upon the surface of the earth not only human beings, but also many different species of plants and animals, etc. etc..

WHAT IS PHILOSOPHY?

One way in which we might get a general description of the whole Universe, is by making additions to the views of Common Sense of the comparatively simple sort which I have just indicated. But many philosophers have held that any such view as this is very incorrect indeed. And different philosophers have held it to be incorrect in three different ways. They have either held that there certainly are in the Universe some most important kinds of things--substantial kinds of things--in addition to those which Common Sense asserts to be in it. Or else they have positively contradicted Common Sense: have asserted that some of the things which Common Sense supposes to be in it, are not in it, or else, that, if they are, we do not know it. Or else they have done both; both added and contradicted.

I wish now to give some examples of all three kinds of views. Both of those which add something very important to the views of Common Sense; and of those which contradict some of the views of Common Sense; and of those which do both.

To begin then with those which add something to the views of Common Sense.

There is, first of all, one view of this type which everybody has heard of. You all know, that enormous numbers of people, and not philosophers only, believe that there certainly is a God in the Universe: that, besides material objects and our acts of consciousness, there is also a Divine Mind, and the acts of consciousness of this mind; and that, if you are to give any complete description of the sum of things, of everything that is, you must certainly mention God. It might even be claimed that this view--the view that there is a God, is itself a view of Common Sense. So many people have believed and still do believe that there certainly is a God, that it might be claimed that this is a Common Sense belief. But, on the other hand, so many people now believe that, even if there is a God, we certainly do not know that there is one; that this also might be claimed as a view of Common Sense. On the whole, I think it is fairest to say, that Common Sense has no view on the question whether we do know that there is a God or not: that it neither asserts that we do know this, nor yet that we do not; and that, therfore, Common Sense has no view as to the Universe as a whole. We may, therefore, say that those philosophers who assert that there certainly is a God in the Universe do go beyond the views of Common Sense. They make a most important addition to what Common Sense believes about the Universe. For by a God is meant something so different both from material objects and from our minds, that to add that, besides these, there is also a God, is certainly to make an important addition to our view of the Universe.

And there is another view of this type, which also everybody has heard of. Everybody knows that enormous numbers of men have believed and still do believe that there is a future life. That is to say, that, besides the acts of consciousness attached to our bodies, while they are alive upon the earth, our minds go on performing acts of consciousness after the death of our bodies --go on performing acts of consciousness not attached to any living body on the surface of the earth. Many people believe that we know this: so many people believe it that, here again as in the case of God, it might be claimed that this is a belief of Common Sense. But, on the other hand, so many people believe that, even if we have a future life, we certainly do not know that we have one; that here again it is perhaps fairest to say that Common Sense has no view on the point: that it asserts neither that we do know of a future life nor that we do not. This, therefore, also may be called an addition to the views of Common Sense; and certainly it is a most important addition. If there really are going on in the Universe at this moment, not only the acts of consciousness attached to the living bodies of men and animals on the surface of this earth, but also acts of consciousness performed by the minds of millions of men, whose bodies have long been dead--then certainly the Universe is a very different place from what it would be, if this were not the case.

Here, then, are two different views of the type which I describe as making important additions to the views of Common Sense, while not contradicting it. And there is only one other view of this type which I wish to mention. Some philosophers have held, namely, that there certainly is in the Universe, something else, beside material objects and our acts of consciousness, and something substantial too--but that we do not know what the nature of this something is--that it is something Unknown or Unknowable. This view, you see, must be carefully distinguished from that which I mentioned above as not going much beyond Common Sense: namely the view that there may be in the Universe, things which are neither material objects nor the acts of consciousness of men and animals, but that we do not know whether there are or not. There is a great difference between saying: There may be in the Universe some other kind of thing, but we do not know whether there is or not; and saying: There certainly is in the Universe some other important kind of thing, though we do not know what it is. This latter view may, I think, fairly be said to go a great way beyond the views of Common Sense. It asserts that in addition to the things which Common Sense asserts to be certainly in the Universe--namely, material objects in Space and the Acts of consiousness attached to living bodies--there certainly is something else besides, though we do not know what this something is. This view is a view which has, I think, been held by people who call themselves Agnostics; but I think it hardly deserves the name. To know, not only that there may be, but that there certainly is in the Universe something substantial besides material objects and our acts of consciousness is certainly to know a good deal. But I think it is a view that is not uncommonly held.

I have given, then, three examples of views which add to Common Sense without contradicting it and I now pass to the second type of views: those which contradict Common Sense, without adding to it; those which deny something which Common Sense professes to know, without professing to know anything, which Common Sense does not profess to know. I will call these, for the sake of a name, sceptical views.

Of this second type, there are, I think, two main varieties, both of which consist in saying that we do not know, certain things which Common Sense says we do know. No views of this type, I think, positively deny that there are in the Universe those things which Common Sense says certainly are in it: they only say that we simply do not know at all whether these things are in it or not; whereas Common Sense asserts quite positively that we do know that they are.

The first variety of this type is that which asserts that we simply do not know at all whether there are any material objects in the Universe at all. It admits that there may be such objects; but it says that none of us knows that there are any. It denies, that is to say, that we can know of the existence of any objects, which continue to exist when we are not conscious of them, except other minds and their acts of consciousness.

And the second view goes even further than this. It denies also that we can know of the existence of any minds or acts of consciousness except our own. It holds, in fact, that the only substantial kind of thing which any man can know to be in the Universe is simply his own acts of consciousness. It does not deny that there may be in the Universe other minds and even material objects too; but it asserts that, if there are, we cannot know it. This is, of course, an illogical position; since the philosopher who holds it, while asserting positively that no man can know of the existence of any other mind, also positively asserts that there are other men beside himself, who are all as incapable as he is of knowing the existence of any one else. But though it is illogical, it has been held. And it would cease to be illogical, if, instead of asserting that no man knows of the existence of any other mind, the philosopher were to confine himself to the assertion that he personally does not.

But now I come to the third type of views--views which depart much further from Common Sense than any that I have mentioned yet; since they both positively deny that there are in the Universe certain things, which Common Sense asserts certainly are in it, and also positively assert that there are in it certain kinds of things, which Common Sense does not profess to know of. Views of this type are, I may say, very much in favour among philosophers.

The chief views of this type may, I think, be divided into two classes: first, those whose contradiction of Common Sense merely consists in the fact that they positively deny the existence of space and material objects; and secondly, those which positively deny many other things as well. Both kinds, I must insist, do positively deny the existence of material objects; they say that there certainly are no such things in the Universe; not merely, like the sceptical views, that we do not know whether there are or not.

First, then, for those views which merely contradict Common Sense by denying the existence of space and material objects.

These views all, I think, start by considering certain things, which I will call the Appearances of material objects. And I think I can easily explain what I mean by this. You all know that, if you look at a church steeple from the distance of a mile, it has a different appearance from that which it has, when you look at it from the distance of a hundred yards; it looks smaller and you do not see it in many details which you see when you are nearer. These different appearances which the same material objects may present from different distances and different points of view are very familiar to all of us: there certainly are such things in the Universe, as these things which I call Appearances of material objects. And there are two views about them, both of which might be held quite consistently with Common Sense, and between which, I think, Common Sense does not pronounce. It might be held that some, at least, among them really are parts of the objects,[1] of which they are appearances: really are situated in space, and really continue to exist, even when we are not conscious of them. But it might also be held, quite consistently with Common Sense, that none of these appearances are in space, and that they all exist only so long as they appear to some one: that, for instance, the appearance which the church tower presents to me on a particular occasion, exists only so long as I see it, and cannot be said to be in the same space with any material object or to be at any distance from any material object. Common Sense, I think, does not contradict either of those views. All that it does insist on, I think, is that these appearances are appearances of material objects—of objects which do exist, when we are not conscious of them, and which are in space. Now the philosophers whose views I am now considering have, I think, all accepted the second of the two views about appearances, which I said were consistent with Common Sense—namely the view that these appearances only exist, so long as the person to whom they appear is seeing them, and that they are not in space. And they have then gone on to contradict Common Sense, by adding that these appearances are not appearances of material objects—that there are no material objects, for them to be appearances of.

And there are two different views of this kind, which have been held.

The first is the view of one of the most famous of English philosophers, Bishop Berkeley. Berkeley's view may, I think, be said to have been that these Appearances are in fact not Appearances of anything at all. He himself says, indeed, that these Appearances are themselves material objects—that they are what we mean by material objects. He says that he is not denying the existence of matter, but only explaining what matter is. But he has been commonly held to have denied the existence of matter, and, I think, quite rightly. For he held that these Appearances do not exist except at the moment when we see them; and anything of which this is true can certainly not properly be said to be a material object: what we mean to assert, when we assert the existence of material objects, is certainly the existence of something which continues to exist even when we are not conscious of it. Moreover he certainly held, I think, that these appearances were not all of them in the same space: he held, for instance, that an appearance, which appears to me, was not at any distance or in any direction from an appearance which appears to you: whereas, as I have said, we should, I think, refuse to call anything a material object, which was not at some distance, in space, in some direction from all other material objects. I think, then, it may fairly be said that Berkeley denies the existence of any material objects, in the sense in which Common Sense asserts their existence. This is the way in which he contradicts Common Sense. And the way in which he adds to it, is by asserting the existence of a God, to whom, he thinks, there appear a set of appearances exactly like all of those which appear to us.

But Berkeley's view has not, I think, been shared by many other philosophers. A much commoner view is that these things which I have called the appearances of material objects, are in fact the appearances of something, but not, as Common Sense asserts, of material objects, but of minds or conscious beings. This view, therefore, both contradicts Common Sense, by denying the existence of material objects, and also goes beyond it by asserting the existence of immense numbers of minds, in addition to those of men and of animals. And it insists, too, that these minds are not in space: it is, it says, not true that they are at any distance in any direction from one another; they are, in fact, all simply nowhere, not in any place at all.

These views are, I think, startling enough. But there are other philosophers who have held views more startling still--who have held not only that space and material objects do not really exist, but also that time and our own conscious acts do not really exist either: that there are not really any such things in the Universe. At least, this is, I think, what many philosophers have meant. What they say is that all these four kinds of things, material objects, space, our acts of consciousness and time, are Appearances; that they are all of them Appearances of something else--either of some one thing, or else some collection of things, which is not a material object, nor an act of consciousness of ours, and which also is not in space nor yet in time. And, as you see, this proposition is ambiguous: whether it contradicts Common Sense or not depends on the question what these philosophers mean by calling these things Appearances. They might conceivably mean that these Appearances were just as real, as the things of which they are appearances; by asserting that they are Appearances of something else, they might only mean to assert that there is in the Universe something else besides—something to which these things are related in the same sort of way in which the appearance of a church-tower, which I see when I look at it from a distance, is related to the real church-tower. And, if they did only mean this, their views would merely be of the type of those that add to Common Sense: they would merely be asserting that, in addition to the things which Common Sense believes to be in the Universe, there is also something else beside or behind these things. But it seems to me quite plain that they do not really mean this. They do mean to maintain that matter and space and our acts of consciousness and time are not real in the sense in which Common Sense believes them to be real, and in which they themselves believe that the something else behind Appearances is real. And holding this, it seems to me that what they really mean is that these things are not real at all: that there are not really any such things in the Universe. What, I think, they really mean (though they would not all admit that they mean it) is something like this. There is a sense in which the pole-star, when we look at it, appears to be much smaller than the moon. We may say, then, that what appears—the appearance, in this case—is simply this: that the pole-star is smaller than the moon. But there simply is no such thing in the Universe as this which appears: the pole-star is not smaller than the moon: and, therefore, what appears to be in the Universe—namely, that it is smaller than the moon—is a simple nonentity—there is no such thing. It is in this sense, I think, that many philosophers have believed and still believe that not only matter and space but also our acts of consciousness and time simply do not exist: that there are no such things. They have believed that they are something which appears; but that what appears simply is not anything—that there is no such thing in the Universe.

This, I think, is what they really mean, though they would not all admit that they mean it. And as to what they hold to be in the Universe, <u>instead of</u> the things which Common Sense holds to be in it, they have held different views. Some have held that it is a collection of different minds; others that it is one mind; others that it is something which is in some sense mental or spiritual, but which cannot be properly said either to be one mind or many.

These, then, are some of the views which have been held as to the nature of the Universe as a <u>whole</u>. And I hope these examples have made clear the sort of thing I mean by the first problem of philosophy--<u>a general</u> description of the whole Universe. Any answer to the problem must consist in saying one or other of three things: it must say <u>either</u> that certain large classes of things are the <u>only</u> kinds of things in the Universe, i.e., that everything in it belongs to one or other of them; or else it must say that everything in the Universe is of one kind; or else it must say that everything which we <u>know</u> to be in the Universe belongs to some one of several classes or to some one class. And it must also, if it holds that there are several different classes of things, say something about the relation of these classes to one another.

This, then, is the first and most interesting problem of philosophy. And it seems to be that a great many others can be defined as problems bearing upon this one.

---

1. I should now say 'parts of the <u>surfaces</u> of the objects'. (1952).

VII.   DEFENDING   COMMOM   SENSE*

NORMAN MALCOLM

-Susan Linn Professor of Philosophy and
Chairman of Philosophy at Cornell Univeristy.

IN "A DEFENCE OF COMMON SENSE"[1] G.E. Moore wrote down a list of propositions which he called "truisms." The following are some of the propositions in that list: "There exists at present a living human body, which is my body"; "The earth had existed for many years before my body was born"; "Ever since it was born it has been either in contact with or not far from the surface of the earth"; "I am a human being"; "I have often perceived both my own body and other things which formed part of its environment, including other human bodies." Moore said that every one of the propositions in his list "I know, with certainty, to be true."[2]

In his "Proof of an External World"[3] Moore gave what he considered to be "a perfectly rigorous proof" of the existence of "things outside of us."[4] He said that he could prove that two human hands exist. "How? By holding up my two hands, and saying, as I make a certain gesture with the right hand, 'Here is one hand,'

*Reprinted with permission of the author and The Philosophical Review, Vol. 58 (1949).

and adding, as I make a certain gesture with the left, 'and here is another.'"⁵ He said that this would not have been a proof unless (among other things) "the premiss which I adduced was something which I <u>knew</u> to be the case, and not merely something which I believed but which was by no means certain, or something which, though in fact true, I did not know to be so." But, he continued,

> I certainly did at the moment <u>know</u> that which I expressed by the combination of certain gestures with saying the words, 'there is one hand and here is another.' I <u>knew</u> that there was one hand in the place indicated by combining a certain gesture with my first utterance of 'here' and that there was another in the different place indicated by combining a certain gesture with my second utterance of 'here.' How absurd it would be to suggest that I did not know it, but only believed it, and that perhaps it was not the case! You might as well suggest that I do not know that I am now standing up and talking --that perhaps after all I'm not, and that it's not quite certain that I am.⁶

Again: "I <u>do</u> know that I held up two hands above this desk not very long ago. As a matter of fact in this case you all know it too. There's no doubt whatever that I did."⁷ Again: "I have, no doubt, conclusive evidence for asserting that I am not now dreaming; I have conclusive evidence that I am awake...."⁸

    I wish to put forward the contention that there is something wrong with Moore's assertions. What I have to say, however, will not be in support of the philosophers who have argued that it is not certain that the earth has existed for many years, or that Moore did not know for certain that he was a human being, or that it is not perfectly certain that he held up a hand during his lecture to the British Academy.

    What then is it which, according to me, is wrong with Moore's assertions? I believe that, in two essays from which I quoted, Moore <u>misused</u> the expressions "I know," "I know with certainty," "It is certain," "I have conclusive evidence." I wish to show that Moore's use of those expressions, as illustrated in those essays, is contrary to their ordinary and correct use.

Moore said that he <u>knew</u> that the statement "Here's a hand," which he uttered as he held up his hand before the audience at his British Academy lecture, was true. That assertion implies that it would have been correct for him to have said, at a time when he and his audience had a clear view of his hand, "I know that here's a hand." At this moment I am holding a pen, there is a desk before me, I am seated in a chair, and through the window I see a near-by tree. Let us imagine that there is another person in this room who has a clear view of me seated in this chair, before this desk, with this pen in my hand, and who has an unobstructed view of that near-by tree. Moore's assertion implies that it would be correct for me to say to that person "I know that I am holding a pen," "I know with certainty that I am sitting in a chair and before a desk," "It's perfectly certain that that (pointing at the tree) is a tree." I contend that I should misuse language if I were to make any of these statements.

Consider the sentence "It's perfectly certain that that is a tree." If we are walking on a meadow in a heavy fog and a tall, indistinct object looms ahead, and one of us wonders whether it is a tree or a telephone pole, it would be a natural thing for one of us to say, "It's perfectly certain that that is a tree, because if you look carefully you will see the faint outline of the branches on either side." That is one example of circumstances in which the sentence "It's perfectly certain that that is a tree" would be correctly used, although it might not be <u>true</u> that that object was a tree. Whether or not it was a tree could be determined by walking closer to it. Consider another example: We are seated in the audience at an open-air theatre, the stage of which is bordered by trees. The stage scenery is painted to represent a woodland, and the painting is so skillfully executed that we are in doubt as to whether that which we see on one side of the stage is a real tree or a painted tree. Finally one of us exclaims "I know that that is a real tree, because just now I saw the leaves move in the breeze." This would be a natural use of language. If a doubt remained as to whether it was a real tree the matter could be finally settled by approaching nearer to the stage. Consider still another example: We are examining an elder plant and the question arises as to whether it is properly called a "tree" or a "shrub." One of us says, "I know that that's a tree because I heard a botany professor say that elders are 'trees' and not 'shrubs.'" Whether or not it is proper to call it a "tree" could be determined by consulting an authoritative book on plants.

Three cases have been described in which it would be a correct use of language, although it might be false, to say, "I know that that's a tree:; and innumerable other cases could be given. Let us notice some features common to these three cases: (1) There is in each case a question at issue and a doubt to be removed. (2) In each case the person who asserts "I know that that's a tree" is able to give a reason for his assertion. (3) In each case there is an investigation which, if it were carried out, would settle the question at issue. I wish to show that all these features are missing when Moore says in a philosophical context "I know that that's a tree."

(1) Consider the circumstances in which, according to Moore, he would have spoken correctly if he had said, during his British Academy lecture, "I know that here is a hand." He and his audience had a clear view of his hand. If his hand had been concealed in a bag it is unlikely that he would have pointed at the bag and said to his audience "I know that here is a hand." Or if it had been rumored that Moore had an artificial hand which closely resembled a human hand, it is likely that he would have changed the example. Perhaps he would have pointed at his head and said, "It's certain that this is a head." The point is that he would have chosen to utter the sentence "I know that here is a hand" in circumstances where there was not even any *question* as to whether there was a hand where he pointed! This feature alone of his use of the sentence "I know that here is a hand" would mark it as not an ordinary use of that sentence. If Moore was having a discussion with someone who had produced an argument in favor of saying that it is never certain that any perceptual judgment is true, Moore would point at a tree which stood close by in plain view of both of them and declare "It's perfectly certain that that is a tree." He would not choose circumstances for uttering that sentence in which the outline of the tree was obscured by heavy fog; or in which there was any question as to whether the thing at which

he pointed was a real tree and not a section of painted scenery, or a real tree and not a mirror image of a tree; or in which there was any question as to whether it was properly called a "tree" or a "shrub." He would pick circumstances for saying "It's perfectly certain that that's a tree" or "I <u>know</u> that that's a tree" in which there was no question at all as to whether the thing at which he pointed was a tree.

The first respect, therefore, in which Moore's usage of the expression "I know," in the philosophical contexts which we are considering, departs from ordinary usage is that Moore says "I know that so and so is true" in circumstances where no one doubts that so and so is true and where there is not even any question as to whether so and so is true. It will be objected: "His opponent has a philosophical doubt as to whether so and so is true, and there is a philosophical question as to whether so and so is true." That is indeed the case. What I am saying is that the philosophical doubt and the philosophical question are raised in circumstances in which there isn't any <u>doubt</u> and isn't any <u>question</u> as to whether so and so is true. Moore's opponent would not raise a philosophical question as to whether it is certain that an object before them is a tree if the object were largely obscured or too distant to be easily seen. If he said "I wish to argue that it isn't certain that that object is a tree" and Moore replied "I can't tell at this distance whether it is a tree or a bush," then Moore's opponent would <u>change the example</u>. He would not want to use as an example for his philosophical argument an object with regard to which there was some doubt as to whether it was a tree. The use of an object as an example for presenting his philosophical doubt is spoiled for him if there <u>is</u> any doubt as to what the object is. It must be the case that there is no doubt that the given object is a tree <u>before</u> he can even raise a philosophical question as to whether it is certain that it is a tree.

It will be objected, "Moore's opponent may truly doubt that the object is a tree in the respect that he may be in doubt as to whether he is dreaming." It is indeed the case that one of the most powerful arguments for the view that the truth of no perceptual judgment is ever certain is the argument used by Descartes for the purpose of proving that one can never know for certain that one is not dreaming. Suppose that we were watching Descartes through the window of his room while he wrote down that argument which produced in him an astonishment "such that it is almost capable of persuading me that I now dream." Suppose that we saw him facing the fire, sometimes placing a fresh log on it, sometimes placing a kettle to boil, as he formulated the considerations which aroused in him that "astonishment." Wouldn't it be unnatural to say in such a case that Descartes was "in doubt" as to whether there was a fire, even if we heard him exclaim, "Perhaps I dream and there is no fire here"? Compare that situation with one in which we are watching through the window a man seated in a room whose view of the fire is cut off by a screen. Twice the fire has gone out and he has started it again, and frequently now he lays down his writing in order to peer over the screen. It would be natural to say in such a case that each time he rose to peer over the screen he was in doubt as to whether there was a fire. The sort of circumstances in which it would be unnatural to say of a man that he "doubts" that there is a fire are the very circumstances in which that man might express a philosophical doubt as to whether there is a fire!

Consider this case: A man awakes from sleep and sees a fire burning brightly in the grate. He is astonished because he has no recollection of having started a fire. He shakes his head as if to rouse himself, stares hard at the fire, says, "Perhaps I dream and there is no fire," dashes cold water in his face and looks at the fire again, walks to it with hand extended to feel its warmth, and, continuing to express astonishment, calls in his neighbor from the next apartment, to whom he addresses the question "Am I dreaming, or do I really see a fire?"

This man is in doubt as to whether he is dreaming or awake, in the ordinary sense of those words. His doubt is expressed in <u>actions</u> of doubting. When a man is entertaining a philosophical doubt as to whether he is dreaming or awake he does not perform actions of that sort. We must not understand this to mean merely that he does not, <u>in fact</u>, perform actions of that sort, although he <u>could</u> do so. The truth is that if he did perform actions of that sort then we should no longer say that he was entertaining a philosophical doubt. The very actions which would count in favor of saying that he was <u>in doubt</u> as to whether he was awake would count <u>against</u> saying that he was feeling a philosophical doubt.

It will be said that Moore's philosophical opponent may be in doubt as to whether he is seeing a real tree or is instead suffering from hallucination. Let us consider the sort of circumstances in which I (or any philosopher) should give utterance to a philosophical doubt as to whether I was having a hallucination. I should fix my eyes upon some object in plain view at close range, such as the chair in that corner. I should say or think "How do I know that I see a chair? Perhaps I am having a hallucination. Perhaps I am really looking at a dog and because of my hallucination it seems to me that I see a chair." I should turn over in my mind one or more of the several philosophical arguments which have been offered to prove that it is never absolutely certain that one is not having a hallucination. If as I looked at that chair it should suddenly turn into a dog, or seem to, then I should be enormously startled. I should think "Is this a hallucination? Is it a dog I see?" I should be apprehensive of the thing in the corner. I should look about me with anxiety to see whether anything else in the room presented an unusual appearance. I should have ceased my philosophical reflection. I should have been jarred out of my philosophical doubt! I should be <u>in doubt</u>, in the ordinary sense of the words, as to whether I was having a hallucination. If I said "Do I really see a dog or is this hallucination?" I should <u>not</u> now be expressing a philosophical doubt. If the thing in the corner continued to look and behave and sound like a dog, and if everything else around me looked entirely normal, then I should begin to feel confident that it was really a dog I saw. And if my wife, when I called her in, should express astonishment at there being a dog there, then it would be a natural thing for me to say "I thought for a moment that perhaps I was having a hallucination or was dreaming. Now I know that I'm not. It really is a dog!" Once I was perfectly reassured that I was not having a hallucination, then I could resume my philosophical reflection--that is, I could proceed again to entertain a philosophical doubt as to whether I was having a hallucination.

Let us compare the natural use of the sentence "I know that I'm not dreaming or having a hallucination," which we have just described, with Moore's philosophical use of it. One feature of the circumstances of its natural use was that something <u>extraordinary</u> had occurred. Another feature was that <u>my anxiety</u> as to whether I was suffering from hallucination or had actually seen a chair turn into a dog, expressed itself in such actions as rising from my chair in alarm, glancing apprehensively about me, scrutinizing closely the thing in the corner, calling in my wife. Another feature was that as a result of performing those actions my anxiety and doubt were removed. Now consider the circumstances in which Moore, in his British Academy lecture, said "I have, no doubt, conclusive reasons for asserting that I am not now dreaming; I have conclusive evidence that I am awake...."[9] Nothing extraordinary had occurred. Neither he nor anyone present had any doubt about it. There was not even any <u>question</u> as to whether he was dreaming. Yet in those circumstances Moore uttered the sentence "I have conclusive evidence that I am awake." Ordinarily a statement like that would be made only if there was some reason to think that he was dreaming, and only if he or someone else felt a doubt about it, and only if he had done something to remove the doubt. None of these things are true of the circumstances in which Moore made his statement. His use of the sentence "I have conclusive evidence that I am awake" was an enormous departure from ordinary usage.

With respect to the objection, therefore, that Moore's philosophical opponent does have a doubt as to whether he really sees a tree or is, instead, dreaming or having an hallucination, it should be answered: Moore's opponent has a <u>philosophical</u> doubt as to whether he is dreaming, but this does not imply that he is <u>in doubt</u> as to whether he is dreaming. To call a philosophical doubt <u>a doubt</u> is as misleading as to call a rhetorical question a <u>question</u>. We should not say that a man was feeling a philosophical doubt as to whether he was having an hallucination if he was, <u>in the ordinary sense of the words</u>, in doubt as to whether he was having an hallucination. Nor should we say that he was raising a philosophical question as to whether he might not be dreaming if the circumstances were such that there <u>was</u> some question as to whether he was dreaming.

(2) The second thing that we noticed about the natural use of the sentence "I know that that is a tree" is that the person who utters it is able to support his assertion with a <u>reason</u>. Suppose that we were on the top of a high hill and we were curious as to whether something which we saw in the valley below was a tree or a shrub. If one of us said "I know that it is a tree," it would be natural to ask "How do you know?" This question is a request for a reason, for proof, for evidence. Many different reasons might be given, e.g., "I was down at that place yesterday and remember seeing a tree there"; or "If you will compare the height of it with that of the barn nearby you will see that it must be a tree." If the person answered our question with "I have no reason or "I have a reason but I don't know what it is," we should think it rather queer. We should think that he should not have said, "I know that that is a tree" but should have said instead, "I am inclined to believe that that is a tree but I have no reason for it." We should feel that the use of the word "know," unaccompanied by a reason, was inappropriate.

Now a striking thing about Moore's utterance, in a philosophical context, of a statement like "I know that that is a tree," is that he cannot offer any reason in support of his statement. In his British Academy lecture he said: "How am I to prove now that 'Here's one hand, and here's another'? I do not believe I can do it. In order to do it, I should need to prove for one thing, as Descartes pointed out, that I am not now dreaming. But how can I prove that I am not? I have, no doubt, conclusive reasons for asserting that I am not now dreaming; I have conclusive evidence that I am awake: but that is a very different thing from being able to prove it. I could not tell you what all my evidence is; and I should require to do this at least, in order to give you a proof."[10] He insisted, however that "I can know things, which I cannot prove...."[11] In "A Defence of Common Sense" he said, "But do I really <u>know</u> all the propositions in (1) to be true?" ("(1)" is the list of propositions such as "there exists at present a living human body, which is <u>my</u> body," "the earth had existed for many years before my body was born," "I am a human being," etc.). "Isn't it possible that I merely believe them? or know them to be highly probable? In answer to this question, I think I have nothing better to say than that it seems to me that I do know them, with certainty....We are all, I think, in this strange position that we do <u>know</u> many things, with regard to which we <u>know</u> further that we must have had evidence for them, and yet we do not know <u>how</u> we know, i.e., we do not know what the evidence <u>was</u>."[12]

Moore's remark, "I can know things which I cannot prove," possesses on the surface of it a certain plausibility. In ordinary life circumstances do occur in which we should say that someone knew that so and so was true although he could not prove it. I might know, for example, that Mr. R. entered the apartment house on the night of the crime. If the district attorney asked, "How do you know?" I might reply, "I saw him." If the district attorney asked, "How do you know that it was Mr. R. you saw?" I might reply, "Because I had a clear, close view of his face." If my testimony was doubted, I might prove that Mr. R. did enter the apartment house that night by producing several reliable witnesses to testify that they too saw him enter it. If, however, I was not able to produce those other witnesses, because they were all dead, I would not be able to prove it, although I knew it. In this case there was something which the district attorney would have called proof <u>if</u> I could have produced it.

The philosophical context in which Moore would say "I know that that is a tree" is very dissimilar. Although Moore's opponent asks "How do you know that that is a tree?" there is nothing which he would <u>call</u> a proof that it is a tree. There is not even anything which he would call a <u>reason</u> for saying that it is a tree. It would be pointless for Moore to say to him, "I know that it is a tree because I see that it is a tree"; or to say "I know that it is a tree because I have a clear, close view of it." In the philosophical context these remarks would be utterly irrelevant. If Moore were to say, "I know that I do see a tree and am not suffering from hallucination, because just now I saw my wife point at the place I am looking and heard her say 'I must trim that tree,'" the philosophical reply would be, "That is no reason, because it may be part of your hallucination that you saw and heard your wife." There is nothing at all which Moore could offer in defense of his statement "I know that that is a tree." There is nothing which in that context would be called "proof" or "reason" or "evidence" for that statement. It follows from this that Moore's use of "know" in that context is a departure from its ordinary use. In ordinary discourse we are reluctant to say that someone <u>knows</u> that so and so is true if he cannot give some reason or some evidence for saying that so and so is true. If he can offer no reason or evidence at all then we are inclined to say that he should not have said that he <u>knew</u> that so and so is true. Moore's philosophical usage of "know" breaks this connection between the ordinary use of the word "know" and the being able to give a <u>reason</u>.

It also breaks the connection between the ordinary use of the word "know" and the being able to give a <u>proof</u>. Let me make this clearer. As was noted before, we do permit it to be said, in some circumstances, that a person knows something which he cannot prove. He <u>may</u> know that that thing at the base of the cliff is a tree, and not a bush, because he says that he was down there a month ago; but he cannot <u>prove</u> that it is a tree because the recent landslide prevents those who doubt his word from climbing to the bottom and seeing for themselves whether it is a tree. We all understand perfectly well, however, that there is something which we should call a proof. If by some extraordinary feat we <u>were</u> able to descend, then his assertion would be proved or disproved, because then we should have a close view of the thing. His claim would have been proved true or false, depending on the outcome.

In the philosophical context the difficulty in the way of proving that the thing at which we are looking is a tree is not that none of the procedures of proof appropriate to normal contexts of doubt can, in fact, be carried out. The difficulty is that there is no procedure whatever which, even if it were carried out, would be called a "proof" that the thing we see is a tree. In this context there is not, therefore, a <u>concept</u> of proof. In ordinary discourse the statement, "I know it, although I cannot prove it," is made in circumstances where there is a concept of proof, but where a proof cannot, <u>as a</u>

matter of fact, be obtained. In the philosophical context anyone who says "I know it is a tree, although I cannot prove it" is trying to fit the concept of knowledge into a context in which there is no concept of proof. To try to divorce in this way the concept of knowledge from the concept of proof is a radical violation of the logic of ordinary language.

(3) These last remarks pertain to the third feature of the ordinary use of "I know that so and so"--namely, that in any particular context in which it is used there is an investigation which would settle whether "So and so" is true. Let us take as an example the sentence "I know that I see a hand." It will be helpful to consider some of the different contexts in which the words "Is that a hand I see?" might be uttered:

(a) I see a man standing a thousand yards from me. Some object is thrust above his head. I cannot tell whether it is one of his hands or is some other object. "Is that a hand I see?"

(b) I see a man seated twenty feet away. One of his hands is in plain view. I know that sometimes he wears gloves which are the color of flesh. Perhaps I see the surface of a glove and not the surface of a hand. "Is that a hand I see?"

(c) I am sitting half asleep before the fire. Suddenly I seem to see a hand thrust through the window curtains ten feet away. Am I dreaming? Am I "seeing things"? "Is that a hand I see?"

(d) I know that the man sitting across the table from me has an artificial hand, but I don't remember whether it is his left or his right. One hand of his rests on the table. I am not sure whether it is a hand of flesh and blood or an artificial hand. "Is that a hand I see?"

In each of these cases it would be natural to use the same sentence "Is that a hand I see?" But in each case there is a different question at issue. To each of these different questions a different investigation is appropriate. In (a) I should close the distance to a hundred yards and look again. In (b) I should approach to within three feet and look closely for seams, or lightly pass my finger over part of the surface. In (c) I should rouse myself with a shake of my body, open my eyes wider, look more sharply, change slightly the posture of my head in order to obtain a different angle of vision. In (d) I should reach across and press the hand firmly with my fingers. The actions of investigation, "the ways of finding out," which were suitable in one case would not be suitable in the other cases.

Let us suppose that in each of these cases there is another person to whom I direct the interrogatory sentence, "Is that a hand I see?" and who replies with the declarative sentence "I know that it is a hand." Just as the interrogatory sentence might be said to express in each case a different question, so in each case the declarative sentence might be said to mean something different--to make a different assertion. The sentence "I know that it is a hand" refers to the same question which the interrogatory sentence expresses in that context, and it refers to the investigation which would answer that question. In each context in which the sentence is uttered it refers only to the question and the investigation which belong to that context. In every ordinary context the assertion "I know that it is a hand" implies that there is an appropriate investigation which would, if it were carried out, decide that particular question at issue.

A surprising thing about the philosophical context in which Moore would say "I know that that is a hand" is that his sentence is not connected with any investigation. Moore himself indicated this when he discussed, before the British Academy audience, the difficulty about proving his premises.

> Of course, in some cases what might be called a proof of propositions which seem like these can be got. If one of you suspected that one of my hands was artificial he might be said to get a proof of my proposition 'Here's one hand, and here's another' by coming up and examining the suspected hand close up, perhaps touching and pressing it, and so establishing that it really was a human hand. But I do not believe that any proof is possible in nearly all cases. How am I to prove now that 'Here's one hand, and here's another'? I do not believe I can do it.[13]

Indeed he cannot do it. The reason he cannot is that there is no investigation to be undertaken. If someone in Moore's audience had stood up and said, "Let me feel

87

it; then I shall know whether it is a hand," he would have shown that he did not <u>understand</u> what was going on. His remark would have shown that he did not understand that the question whether anyone knows that it is a hand is a <u>philosophical</u> question. It would be the same if he had proposed any other investigation. He would understand the philosophical nature of the question only if he saw that there was no investigation to be undertaken.

It is inaccurate, therefore, to say, as I said in the preceding paragraph, that Moore "cannot" prove that it is a hand he is holding up. The accurate thing to say is that it does not make sense to ask for a proof in those circumstances. A proof is the result of an investigation. If the context does not allow for an investigation it does not allow for a proof.

I believe that Moore thought that it did make sense to ask for a proof of "Here's a hand" as he stood before his audience, and that he was troubled at not being able to give one. That he thought so is shown from the fact that he was willing to assert, "I <u>know</u> that here's a hand." The ordinary uses of "know" and "proof" are joined in such a way that if it makes sense to assert "I <u>know</u> that so and so is true," it also makes sense to ask for a <u>proof</u> that so and so is true. Thinking that a request for a proof that "Here's a hand" was in that situation a legitimate request, but one he could not satisfy, Moore was led to contend that he knew something which he could not prove. His contention gives aid and comfort to his opponents, the very skeptics whom he wishes to overthrow. For they are inclined to say, "If you cannot prove it then you don't know it." This retort of theirs would be justified if the request for a proof were legitimate. But it isn't. To say "Prove that here's a hand," in circumstances like those in which Moore said that he could not prove that "Here's a hand," is to utter nonsense. There the hand is, right before everyone's eyes; what would it mean to "prove" that it is a hand? The sentence "Prove that here's a hand" has the grammatical form of a request, but in those circumstances it does not <u>function</u> as a request. If the philosopher who says, "Try to prove that here's a hand; you can't do it," doesn't want any of the actions of investigation carried out which are normally carried out in order to satisfy a request for a proof that something we see is a hand, then it is very misleading, if not downright wrong, to say that he is "requesting a proof."

It may be objected: "The philosophical question 'How do I know that this is a hand?' is a request for a **philosophical** investigation, and since it does refer to an investigation the request for a proof is not senseless." It is true that when the question "How do I know that this is a hand?" is asked philosophically it is appropriate to undertake a philosophical investigation. But this investigation is not of a kind which could result in a proof that "Here's a hand." "Investigation" here means something quite different. There are a number of philosophical arguments which seem to prove that it cannot ever be known with absolute certainty, "beyond the possibility of doubt," that any statement like "Here's a hand" is true. The examination of these arguments is a philosophical investigation, and it is a labor of great difficulty and importance. But even if one were to succeed in refuting all of these arguments one would not have proved that "Here's a hand" is true. What we mean by proving that something that we see is a hand is not a philosophical activity. It would be a philosophical activity to show that none of the reasons offered by various philosophers for saying that no one $\underline{can}$ know such a thing as "Here's a hand" are good reasons. One would not have proved thereby that in any particular case when one said, "That's a hand" one was right. Proving the latter would not be doing philosophy at all.

When Moore said, "I cannot prove that 'Here's a hand'" his statement made it seem as if none of the methods of proving such a thing could, as a matter of fact, be carried out. The truth of the case was not, however, that none of the actions and procedures which, in various circumstances, are regarded as methods of proving that a thing we see is a hand, could, as a matter of fact, be carried out. The truth of the case was that all of those actions and procedures were <u>irrelevant</u> to that context! Instead of saying, "I cannot prove that 'Here's a hand,'" it would have been more exact to have said, "This is a situation in which the word 'proof' does not have a correct use." In such circumstances it is neither correct to say, "I cannot prove that that's a hand" nor to say, "I can prove it." Likewise, it is not correct to say, "I know that that's a hand," and not correct to say, "I don't know that that's a hand." It is an essential part of the usage of "know," as well as "prove," that it is joined to an inquiry. The statement "I know that that's a hand," in its ordinary meaning, implies that there is a mode of inquiry, an activity of finding out, a procedure of investigation, which, if it were carried out would result in a proof that "That's a hand." Moore's assertion "I know that 'Here's a hand'" was extraordinary because it did not have that implication. Moore was well aware that it would have been completely pointless for anyone to have brought the hand closer to his eyes or to have pressed it, or to have performed any of the actions of investigation which would be customarily joined to that assertion. In such a case to declare, "I know that 'Here's a hand'" is as eccentric as to labor at turning the crank of an automobile which one knows to be without an engine. If you take away from that sentence its connection with actions of investigation you turn it into an empty utterance.

I am contending that if Moore and I were sitting within a few feet of an apple tree which was in plain view of both of us, it would be a misuse of ordinary language for either of us to point at it and say, "I know that that's a tree." Someone might be inclined to reply, "It would be queer undoubtedly, for either of you to utter that sentence in such a case; but what would make it queer is that it is so obvious to both of you that it is a tree that there is no need to say it! To utter that sentence in those circumstances would be an odd use but not a misuse."

This reply contains a mistake. The mistake lies in the assumption that in those circumstances it would be correct to say "It is obvious that it is a tree." Consider this example: We are looking at something a mile away on the side of a hill and because of the distance and angle of view we cannot make out whether it is a tree or a bush. As we approach it, it more and more distinctly assumes the shape of a tree, until, at a point several hundred yards from it, one of us says "It's perfectly obvious now that it is a tree." This is an ordinary use of those words. In the first place, a doubt existed. The use of those words was to remove the doubt. They were like saying, "You need not have that doubt any longer." In the second place, further investigation would not be unreasonable. If one of us had weak vision and still doubted that it was a tree he could walk closer. There would come a point, still at a considerable distance from the tree, at which he too would say, "Yes, it obviously is a tree."

Suppose now that we should walk right up to the tree and begin to pick apples from it. If one of us should then say, "It's obvious that this is a tree," that would be a mi̲suse of those words and would raise a laugh. In the fi̲r̲s̲t place, no one has any doubt on the matter and the utterance of those words is not fulfilling its normal purpose, which is to remove doubt. In the second place, there is no further investigation which would "back up" those words. Should we pick more apples? Should we take photographs? Should we strip the bark? None of those things would be called "making certain" or "further verifying" or "trying to find out" whether it is a tree. There is nothing which, in those circumstances, we should call "trying to find out whether it is a tree." This means that, in those circumstances, we don't attach any sense to the question "Is it a tree?" We don't know what to d̲o̲ with it. In those circumstances the sentence "It's obvious that it's a tree" is a mi̲s̲f̲i̲t̲. It doesn't be̲l̲o̲n̲g̲ there. It is a set of idle words. It has no function. It has a function only in those contexts where we attach sense to the question "Is it a tree?"

To the argument of this paper the following objection may be made:

> You said that a philosophical question as to whether it is certain that a thing before us is a tree, can be expressed only in circumstances where there isn't any doubt and isn't any question about its being a tree, and that in a philosophical discussion Moore would say, 'I know that that's a tree,' in circumstances where there was no question that the thing at which he pointed was a tree. Now in ordinary language, 'There's no doubt that it is a tree,' or 'There's no question about its being a tree,' are e̲q̲u̲i̲v̲a̲l̲e̲n̲t̲ to 'I know that it's a tree' or 'It's certain that it's a tree.' It follows from your own argument that Moore speaks both correctly and truly when he says, in such a context, 'It's certain that

that's a tree,' and that he does not misuse language in the least.

This objection rests on a misunderstanding of a matter which I am anxious to clarify, and which, I fear, my previous remarks have not sufficiently clarified.

I declared that a man who is entertaining a philosophical doubt as to whether what he sees is a tree does not have any doubt that it is a tree. This statement may easily mislead, because it makes the case appear to be this--that when a man has a philosophical doubt he does not, in fact, have any doubt, although of course he could have a doubt. The truth is that, in the sort of circumstances in which a man expresses a philosophical doubt (and it must be expressed in circumstances of that sort--otherwise we should not call it a philosophical doubt) as to whether, for example, there is really a fire in the grate before him, it is nonsense to say "He doubts that there is a fire." It isn't that, in fact, he doesn't doubt. It is, rather, that it would be a misuse of language to say "He doubts," and, therefore, a misuse of language to say "He doesn't doubt."

My statement, "A man who is expressing a philosophical doubt as to whether there is a fire before him isn't in doubt as to whether there is a fire," is analogous to the statement, "An automobile isn't intelligent." The latter statement doesn't mean that, in fact, automobiles are not intelligent at the present time, although next year's models may be. What it means is expressed more accurately by the statement "To say that 'this automobile is intelligent' or that 'this automobile isn't intelligent' doesn't make sense. It is a misuse of words to say of an automobile that it 'is intelligent' or 'isn't intelligent.'" My statement about the man expressing a philosophical doubt is put more accurately by the statement, "In the circumstances in which a man expresses a philosophical doubt as to whether there is a fire before him it would be a misuse of words to say either 'He doubts' or 'He doesn't doubt' that there is a fire.

If a man who is preparing to cook his dinner on a coal stove touches the stove and finds it hot, puts potatoes in the oven and sits down to wait for them to bake, but doesn't look in the fire compartment to find out whether there is still a fire--then we could say that he "doesn't doubt" or "assumes" or "takes for granted" that there is a fire. If he begins to show concern that the potatoes take so long to bake and tries to open the door to the fire compartment to look inside but can't get it open, then we could say that he "doubts" that there is a fire. It is a feature <u>common</u> to both cases, i.e., the case in which we could say that he "doesn't doubt" and the case in which we could say that he "doubts," that he <u>doesn't see</u> the interior of the fire compartment because of the closed door. But if the door was open and he watched the flames as he waited, while occasionally stirring the fire, then it sould be as grotesque to say that he "doesn't doubt" or that he "assumes" or "takes for granted" or "believes" that there is a fire, as to say that he "doubts" that there is a fire. In this case neither "doubts" nor "doesn't doubt" makes sense.

The objection which opened this section may be answered as follows: When I say that a philosophical doubt as to whether, for example, an object before our eyes is a hand, is expressed in circumstances where there is no doubt that it's a hand, the words "There is no doubt that it's a hand" are not to be understood in the sense in which they are equivalent to "It's certain that it's a hand." What is meant is that in those circumstances a <u>doubt</u> is senseless. Instead of saying, "A philosophical doubt as to whether this thing before me is a hand is expressed in circumstances where there's no doubt that it's a hand," it is more accurate to say "A philosophical doubt as to whether this is a hand is expressed in circumstances where it would be a misuse of language to say <u>either</u> 'There's some doubt that this is a hand' <u>or</u> 'There's no doubt that this is a hand.'" Similarly, instead of saying, "The question 'Is it certain that this is a hand?' is not a philosophical question unless it is asked in circumstances where there's no question that it's a hand," it is more accurate to say "The question 'Is it certain that this is a hand?' is not a philosophical question unless it is asked in circumstances where the question 'Is this a hand?' as ordinarily understood, would be without sense."

I am contending that Moore's philosophical assertions,

such as "I know that here's a hand" or "I know that I am a human being," are made in circumstances where it is a misuse of words to say either "I know that here's a hand" or "I don't know that here's a hand," or to say either "I know that I'm a human being" or "I don't know that I'm a human being." To this the following objection will be made: "Either I know that I am a human being or I don't know it. One or the other <u>must</u> be the case."

If my contention sounds to you like an absurd paradox and this reply seems irrefutable, it is because you have before your mind the normal usage of "I know" and "I don't know." If I see something moving on the top of a distant hill it is true that either I know that it is a human being or I don't know it. In those circumstances we attach sense to the question "Is it a human being?" There is something which we should call "investigating" and "finding out" whether it is or it isn't. This is one of the contexts of the normal usage of "know" and "don't know." In these contexts "I know" is opposed to "I don't know." "Either I know or I don't know" is a rule which applies to these expressions when they occur in their normal contexts. But when these expressions occur in unnatural contexts this rule no longer applies. Consider the sentence, "My desk is good-natured." There is no paradox involved in saying that my desk neither is good-natured nor isn't good-natured. It would be fantastic to insist that either my desk is good-natured or it isn't and that it must be one or the other. We don't attach sense to the words, "Is it a good-natured desk?" There is nothing which we should recognize as an "investigation" into whether it is or it isn't.

Just as "good-natured" does not belong to certain contexts, so "I know" does not belong to certain contexts. If I should come up to you and ask with earnest countenance "Am I a human being?" you would be taken quite aback. It would not be clear to you what my words mean. You would not understand to what investigation they referred. You would not know what <u>sort</u> of thing an "answer" would be. You would be equally perplexed if I should solemnly declare to you, "I <u>know</u> that I'm a human being." My statement would seem to you as strange and outlandish as "My desk isn't good-natured."

There could be circumstances in which "Am I a human being?" would be a question with sense. Suppose that I have fallen from a height and have been knocked unconscious. Gradually I return to consciousness. I am dazed and confused. There is utter darkness, and I cannot feel my body. I dimly recall the fall and wonder if I am now "dead." Am I a spirit? Am I without a body? Or "Am I still a human being?" If I should then begin to feel my body and to sort out my limbs, I might exclaim, "I know that I am still a human being." Here is a usage of "Am I a human being?" and "I know that I am a human being" which has sense. The circumstances in which Moore said "I know that I am a human being" were quite unlike this. In his case there was no "question," no "doubt," and no "investigation." When I maintain that in the circumstances in which he uttered those words, neither "I know that I'm a human being" nor "I don't know that I'm a human being" was correct language, I do not contend against a law of logic.

I hold, therefore, that Moore was not defending "common sense" at all when he declared "I know with certainty" that "There exists at present a living human body which is *my* body," that "The earth had existed many years before this body was born," that "For many of these years large numbers of human bodies had, at every moment, been alive upon it," that "I am a human being." His assertions were made in circumstances where there was no question, as to whether Moore had a body and was a human being, or as to whether the earth had existed before he was born, or as to whether there were other human beings living on it. Moore's assertions do not belong to "common sense," i.e., to ordinary language, at all. They involve a use of "know" which is a radical departure from ordinary usage.

Moore wished to attack all those philosophers who hold views from which it follows that no numan being knows that he is a human being and that no numan being knows any proposition like "here's a hand"to be true. Moore, to his everlasting credit, saw that it would be a misuse of language for him to say (when writing in his study), "I don't know that I'm a human being, " or to say (when holding up his hand in plain view before him), "I don't know that this is a hand."[14] Therefore, he stoutly affirmed,"I *know* that I'm a human being," "I *know* that this is a hand." He did not see that these statements too are a misuse of language.

(Editor's Note: The reader of this essay might want to look at Professor Malcolm's later essay entitled "Moore and Wittgenstein on the Sense of 'I know'" published in his volume of essays called Thought and Knowledge (Ithaca: Cornell University Press, 1977). There Professor Malcolm mentions his conversations with Wittgenstein in 1949 and the influence these conversations had on Wittgenstein's final notebooks, published under the title On Certainty (New York: Harper & Row, 1972). Professor Malcolm also sent a copy of "Defending Common Sense" to G.E. Moore and Moore responded with a lengthy letter-- part of which is published in "Moore and Wittgenstein on the Sense of 'I know;" along with Malcolm's replies.)

---

1. I.J.H. Muirhead, ed., Contemporary British Philosophy, 2d ser.

2. Op cit., p. 244

3. In Proceedings of the British Academy, XXV, 1939.

4. Ibid., p. 295

5. Ibid.

6. Ibid., p. 296

7. Ibid., p. 298

8. Ibid., p. 300

9. Ibid.

10. Ibid., pp. 299-300

11. Ibid., p. 300

12. "A Defence of Common Sense," p. 206.

13. "Proof of an External World," p. 299.

14. Let me warn, if it is necessary, that what Moore "saw" is a controversial matter. Moore might deny that he then saw or that he now sees any such thing.

VIII.   ORDINARY LANGUAGE AND COMMON SENSE*

A. D. WOOZLEY

-was Professor of Moral Philosophy at St. Andrews University, Fellow of All Souls College, Oxford University. He is currently Professor of Philosophy at the University of Virginia.

THAT philosophy has for its task the study of linguistic usage is a view so widely held these days that it has almost reached the canonical status of a platitude. We learn all that, as philosophers, we want to learn about promises, for example, by taking the word 'promise', and examining on the one hand its syntax (e.g. the contrast between 'promising to' and 'promising that') and on the other hand its semantics (e.g. the contrasts between 'I promise' and 'I promised'; between 'I promise' and 'He promises'; between 'I promise' and 'I intend'; etc.). It has been argued by Malcolm in more than one place that Moore's great achievement in philosophy has been to bring out the absurdity of philosophically sceptical paradoxes, and to bring it out by showing how they vio-

*Mind, Volume 62, July, 1953.   Reprinted with permission of Basil Blackwell, Publisher.

late ordinary language. This, it is said, is what Moore was clearly doing in his "Defence of Common Sense" and again in his "Proof of the External World." To be sure, what Moore said he was doing was defending common sense. But Malcolm asserts that common sense and ordinary language are the same thing. His chief criticism of Moore appears to be that having successfully shown how the sceptics are violating ordinary usage by doubting or denying that there are material objects, that this is a hand, and so on, he proceeds to violate ordinary usage himself in saying 'I know that this is a hand'. "Moore's assertions", he says, "do not belong to 'common sense', i.e. to ordinary language, at all. They involve a use of 'know' which is a radical departure from ordinary usage."[1]

Some elucidation is here necessary of the phrase 'ordinary language'.

1. Malcolm has a definition of it (in "Moore and Ordinary Language"[2]), such that an expression is an ordinary expression if it would be used to describe a given situation. It is not necessarily the case that it is used to describe the situation, for the situation may never, or not often, occur. And an expression describes a situation (i) if it describes it correctly, or (ii) if, although it describes it incorrectly, the mistake is an empirical one, which can be empirically put right. E.g. 'The earth is flat' is an ordinary expression.

2. It seems doubtful that Malcolm has consistently stuck to that definition. For example, in Defending Common Sense he uses phrases like 'natural thing to say', where he seems to be meaning that an expression is ordinary if it is the usual one employed (or a usual one to be employed) to describe a given situation whenever the situation is described (which might be very seldom). In this use 'describe' occurs as what has been called a task-word; and this sense of 'ordinary' leaves the question open whether the description is correct, and whether, if false, it is only empirically false.

In this sense of 'ordinary','ordinary' is much more ordinary than in Malcolm's other sense; and it is in this sense that I am using it. It is important to see the difference between the two senses. For in sense 1, the proposition which is the backbone of Malcolm's argument for Moore against the sceptical philosophers in "Moore and Ordinary Language", <u>viz</u>. that no ordinary expression can be self-contradictory, is analytic. But in sense 2, the proposition that no ordinary expression can be self-contradictory, so far from being analytic, could easily be (and maybe is) false.

The questions I want to consider are whether common sense and ordinary language are to be identified as Malcolm suggests, and what is the cogency of philosophical appeal to ordinary language. The answers I shall offer are:
    1. that there is a difference between common sense and ordinary language such that you cannot argue from the absurdity of violating the latter to absurdity in disagreeing with the former.
    2. that reasons can be given why their identification looks plausible--if you do not look too hard.
    3. That the ascriptive, or referential, function of statements is not unlike the use of names; and that this is the way in which it is difficult for an expression, if used as it is ordinarily used, to be wrong.

First the point needs to be made that the notion of ordinary language is far from simple; and consequently that departure from ordinary usage is not to be simply determined. This can be illustrated, I think, by what Malcolm has to say about doubt in his <u>Defending Common Sense</u>. He wishes to distinguish the philosophical doubt which he thinks Moore's opponents express whether this is a hand, that is a tree, etc., from doubt whether this is a hand, that is a tree, etc. Not merely does Malcolm want to make this distinction, but he goes on to make two further claims:
    1. That in circumstances in which a man could have a philosophical doubt, he could not have a doubt--<u>i.e</u>. having a doubt and not having a doubt would be equally out of order.
    2. That to call a philosophical doubt a doubt is as misleading as to call a rhetorical question a question.

In other words, the philosopher who says he doubts that this is a hand is simply misusing language. The reason given why he is misusing language is the familiar one that what would stop anyone else from saying that he doubts this is a hand--being able to touch it, feel its texture, cut it and see blood flow, etc.--would not stop the philosopher from saying that he doubts it is a hand.

Now consider this. When a philosopher says 'I doubt this is a hand', what does he mean?
1. He may mean by 'doubt' something different from what is ordinarily meant; and therefore his statement may not, after all, be incompatible with some other statement, e.g. 'I know this is a hand', which would appear to be a contrary of it.

That is what Malcolm thinks the philosopher means.
2. He may mean by 'doubt' the same as what is ordinarily meant. And in that case, when he says 'I doubt this is a hand' (I assume he is not lying),
   (a) His statement may be false--he may not doubt it at all, although he thinks he does, or
   (b) His statement may be true. What would be a satisfactory criterion of his doubting in a situation in which other people do not? Summarily, if his behaviour in the situation were relevantly different from theirs, we would probably allow that he did doubt. But, supposing his behaviour were not different, should we conclude that he was wrong--that he did not doubt? Not necessarily, for whereas what other people might (but in this case do not) suspect is that what we see is a plaster hand, or a stuffed hand, or a trick done with mirrors, he may suspect it of being a bundle of ideas, or a family of sense-data or a retinal image, etc. You may say that that is an odd thing to suspect, and that it can only be suspected through philosophical confusions. But it has been suspected.

In this situation we may say that the philosopher's doubt is different from other people's doubt, because what would confirm or resolve it is quite different from what would confirm or resolve other people's. But we may not, on that account, say that the meaning of 'doubt' as used by the philosopher is different from its meaning as used by other people; there is no reason, so far, why they should not be just the same; and there is no reason, so far, why in one respect at least--viz. meaning the same by 'doubt'--the philosopher should not be conforming with ordinary usage.

This point could be brought out by comparing the philosopher's use of 'doubt; and the ordinary man's use of 'doubt' with Descartes' two uses of 'dubitare'. It is plausible to say that he did philosophically mean by 'dubitare' something different from what he meant non-philosophically. For his philosophical doubting was something which he could decide to do, as opposed to non-philosophical doubting, which it is hardly appropriate to describe oneself as doing at all, let alone deciding to do. His philosophical doubt was thus a refusal to assent to, to answer Yes to, certain questions until certain conditions were fulfilled--a policy of behaving as if, or pretending that, every proposition was or might be false, until the sufficient conditions of its acceptability were satisfied, when it was to be exempted from the doubt. With regard to this doubt it would have been inappropriate to ask Descartes, when he was practising it: "You say you doubt p. But do you really feel doubtful or uncertain of p?" It could be that, as a result of his philosophically doubting p, Descartes should come genuinely to feel uncertain or doubtful of p. But his doubting p philosophically and his feeling doubtful of p would still have been different. The difference could be summarised by saying that his policy of philosophical doubt was the policy of behaving with regard to the propositions in question as if he felt doubtful of or even disbelieved them.

Now, if Malcolm's remarks on the distinction between the philosophers' doubt and ordinary doubt had been aimed only at Descartes, he would have had a good case. But they clearly were not. He talks of philosophers (in the plural), and he repeatedly refers to "Moore's philosophical opponent", without anywhere suggesting that the phrase uniquely describes Descartes. But it is not at all clear that all philosophers who have said that they doubted propositions of the kind mentioned either said they were adopting a Cartesian policy or were adopting it. What is the evidence that they were not just in the position which, as I suggested, Descartes could have come to through sticking to his policy, viz. the position of doubting (i.e. feeling doubtful of) p? If it is true that theirs is an unusual or extraordinary doubt, it is not on that account true that it is a mistake (or misleading) to call it doubt; nor is it on that account true that they are using 'doubt' in a different sense from other people.

Take another of Malcolm's arguments, this time a criticism of Moore himself for violating ordinary language. Moore said, as he held up his right hand, 'I know this is a hand'. But Malcolm replies that this too is a philosophers' violation of ordinary language, because Moore is saying 'I know...' in a situation in which, for non-philosophers, there is no question at all whether it is a hand or not. But statements of the form 'I know (that)...' have a use only in situations where three conditions are fulfilled:
    (i) there is some question or doubt to be settled;
    (ii) the person making the statement 'I know that ...' has some reason in favour of it, or can prove it;
    (iii) there is some investigation which, if carried out, would settle the question at issue.

In Moore's case none of these conditions is fulfilled. Therefore in saying 'I know this is a hand' Moore is violating ordinary language. It is a case where a question of knowledge does not arise: it is equally wrong for Moore to say that he does know and that he does not know. He is perfectly entitled to say 'This is a hand', but not to say 'I know this is a hand'.

Now I do not accept Malcolm's argument either in this case of 'know' or in the earlier case of 'doubt', because I think we need to make some distinctions with regard to ordinary usage which it seems to me that he fails to make. If we take a statement which is syntactically correct and ask whether its use in a particular situation was that of ordinary language there are at least three things we may be asking, such that if the answer to any one of them is Yes, then it is wrong or highly misleading to say, if the answer to any one of the others is No that the user is violating ordinary language. The three things are quite familiar:
    (a) Was the speaker using the expression with the same meaning (= sense, intension, connotation) as it is ordinarily used?
    (b) Was the speaker in using the expression referring to or calling attention to an object or situation of a kind which is ordinarily referred to in the case of that expression?
    (c) Was the speaker using the expression in circum-

stances in which it is ordinarily used?

Malcolm, in effect, treats the philosopher who doubts whether this is a hand as falling foul of question (a) because 'doubt' in his statement does not mean what it ordinarily means. Even if that were true Malcolm should go on to consider questions (b) and (c)-- where his argument would seem more plausible in the case of the whole sentence 'I doubt this is a hand' than in the case of the word 'doubt' alone. But, as I argued earlier, he has not shown that 'doubt' is being used in a non-ordinary sense; so he has not shown ordinary language to be violated.

Moore, in claiming to know that this is a hand is criticised, in effect, by Malcolm for using 'know' in circumstances in which it would not ordinarily be used, i.e. falling foul of (c) alone. To say that I know this is a hand is a singularly pointless thing to say, if nobody has ever suggested that it was not, or has asked what it was, etc. But if every expression, which is pointless because it is unnecessary is to count as a violation of ordinary language, then a great deal of ordinary language is a violation of ordinary language.

What I have tried to maintain so far is that for somebody to have violated ordinary language he needs at least to have offended against (a) above--i.e. he needs to have used the expression in question in a non-ordinary sense. Malcolm failed to show that the sceptics were using 'doubt' in a non-ordinary sense, and made no attempt to show that Moore was using 'know' in a nonordinary sense. To use an expression in circumstances in which it would not ordinarily be used--because it is pointless, or rude, or hurtful--does not constitute a mis-use of language which has philosophical consequences.

Now for the difference between ordinary language and common sense, which I do not find very easy to bring out, but which I think to be there. It is, of course, true that one can think of many statements in which 'common sense' occurs for which we could not sensibly substitute 'ordinary language'--e.g. "It's simply a matter of pure common sense", "Where's you common sense?" "Common sense tells you that the thinner the ice, the more dangerous it is to skate." But I do not think this technique of the substitution-game is any use here, because it is one of a different and more abstract level than the notion of ordinary language--which might still leave it the case that they were not essentially different from each other.

Nevertheless I think they are different. If you are doing what Moore said he was doing, i.e. defending common sense, you are defending beliefs, which to be beliefs of common sense do not necessarily have to be formulated. We all of us believe any number of things which few of us have formulated. Now the beliefs of common sense can be divided into (a) those at a matter-of-fact level: this is a chair, as opposed to a table--a golf ball, as opposed to a rackets ball--a flesh and blood hand, as opposed to a plaster hand, and so on. (b) Those at a metaphysical level: this is an independently existing object, as opposed to a group of God's ideas--I see things as they are, as opposed to a version of things altered by a complicated physiological process, and so on.

One could be wrong about beliefs of either kind. What Moore said was that we could be right, and could be obviously right. I am not quite sure which kind of belief he was talking about: it would seem natural now to say the second; but I am not sure that the distinction between the two kinds had been clearly made by the sceptics or by Moore in his attack on them.

To be defending common sense then is to be defending beliefs, no matter who holds them, no matter whether they have been formulated--although, for a particular belief to be defended, it must, of course, have been formulated. To be defending ordinary language, on the other hand, is to be defending what people say (or would say) in given circumstances. By 'what they say' I mean not 'the view which they express' (this would identify common sense and ordinary language), but 'the way they say what they say' 'the language they use to say what they say'. Now against what kind of charge can one defend ordinary language? You defend a belief of common sense against the charge of being false, or insufficiently substantiated. But if you take what is agreed to be an expression of ordinary language, what is the charge against it to be? Not that it is false, but that it is out of place here--e.g. because, although it is ordinarily used, it is not ordinarily used to apply to a situation of this kind, or because, although it is ordinarily used to apply to a situation of this kind, it is not ordinarily used to apply to a situation of this kind in circumstances of this kind.

The contrast between ordinary language and common sense can perhaps be brought out in this way, by contrasting the statement
   (i) This (is what) is called a hand,
and the statement
   (ii) This is a hand.
(i) is a statement about ordinary language, about the way an expression in it is used. (ii) is not a statement about ordinary language at all, but an example of ordinary language, and might serve as the expression of a common sense belief. But we would consider it differently, according as we were asking a question about ordinary language or about common sense. In the first case, we are asking whether it is the (a) correct expression to use here, and corresponding to statement (i) we have the question "Is this (what is) called a hand?" In the second case, we are not asking a linguistic question at all, but a question corresponding to statement (ii) "Is this a hand?"

To know whether this is called a hand I need not know much about hands, indeed in principle I need not know anything about them at all beyond the semantic fact that people do (would) call this a hand. To know whether it is a hand I do need to know something about hands, not much perhaps but something. In the example I have used both questions might fairly be called empirical, but if we change the example and substitute 'independently existing object', then (i) "Is this (what is) called an independently existing object?" is still an empirical question but (ii) "Is this an independently existing object?" may not be an empirical question--at least if we mean by an empirical question one which is to be answered by further looking, listening, etc. A given statement then may at once be an ordinary language statement and a common sense statement, and, as the latter, may be either empirical or not; but its being an ordinary language statement is different from its being a common sense statement. Whether Moore has been doing what he said he was doing, defending common sense, or what Malcolm first said he was doing, defending ordinary language, he has not been doing what Malcolm second said he was doing, defending both because they are the same thing, because they are not the same thing.

*   *   *

---

1. "Defending Common Sense," Phil. Rev., 1949, p. 219.

2. The Philosophy of G.E. Moore, ed., Schilpp, pp. 345-368

IX.   METAPHYSICS   AND   COMMON

SENSE*

ALFRED JULES AYER

-was Wykeham Professor of Logic in the University of Oxford, Fellow of New College, Oxford. He is a Fellow of the British Adacemy and a Fellow at Wolfson College, Oxford.

If we go by appearances, it can hardly be disputed that metaphysics is nearly always in conflict with common sense. This is most obvious in the case of the metaphysician who professes to find a logical flaw, a contradiction or a vicious infinite regress, in one or other of the ways in which we commonly describe the world, and so comes to such startling conclusions as that time and space are unreal, or that nothing really moves, or that there are not many things in the Universe but only one, or that nothing which we perceive through our senses is real or wholly real, or that there is no such thing as matter, or no such things as minds. It is, however, also true of those who maintain not that the features which common sense ascribes to the external world are unreal, but that they are dependent upon our consciousness of them, that space and time are merely forms of human

*Copyrighted in 1966 by A.J. Ayer and used with his permission.

intuition, or that none of the things which we classify as physical objects exist except when they are being perceived, or that the world is my idea. Even philosophers who wish to dissociate themselves from metaphysics often advance theories which are shocking to common sense, as that there are no private experiences, or that everything that exists is constructed out of sense-data, or that no one ever does anything of his own free will, or that the past is determined by the future as much as the future by the past.

In the eyes of many contemporary philosophers, the fact that such assertions do conflict with common sense is sufficient to condemn them. This is something of a new departure in the history of philosophy, where common sense has not on the whole been treated with very much respect. It is mainly due to the work of G.E. Moore who looked at metaphysics with the devastating simplicity and candour of the child in the Hans Anderson story of the Emperor's Clothes. His technique was to take metaphysical assertions at their face value and show how extraordinary their implications were. Thus he pointed out that if time is unreal, it follows that nothing ever changes or decays or grows, that a man's birth does not precede his death, and indeed that almost every would-be empirical proposition is false, since they nearly all imply that something happens before or after or simultaneously with something else. If matter is unreal, then the stars and the sun and the earth and everything in it, including human beings themselves, are as mythical as unicorns or gorgons. It follows also that if such theories are true, nobody holds them. For if matter is unreal, there are no metaphysicians: and if time is unreal, then nobody ever makes a statement or acquires a belief.

So again, if the world is my idea, it follows that it came into existence with my birth and will disappear at my death; if things exist only when they are perceived, then unless we rely on the perpetual vigilance of a problematic deity, we have to conclude that they are constantly popping in and out of existence, as well as holding that there never has been and never will be a time at which the Universe fails to contain sentient beings; if space and time are merely forms of human sensibility, it follows that the Universe is co-terminous with the existence of the human race. This result may not be quite so ludicrous as that of holding that space and time are unreal. But can any sane man seriously believe it?

Now it might be expected that the defenders of such metaphysical positions would have made some attempt to protect themselves against this sort of treatment, and in some cases they have done so. In the case of those whom Moore was especially attacking, the English neo-Hegelians like Bradley and MacTaggart who maintained the unreality of matter and of space and time, the line taken was to mitigate the charge of unreality; things which were not ultimately real might nevertheless be real as appearances. In this way an attempt was made to give common sense its due: it was able and entitled to distinguish between reality and illusion at its own level, the level of appearances, and the same would apply to science which was, indeed, only a sophistication of common sense. But the metaphysician was bound to go deeper, to probe for the more genuine reality which lay beneath the appearances, and this was discovered to be very different; so different that the most central concepts which served for the description of appearances were wholly inapplicable to it.

The trouble with this defence is that it is hardly more than a sham. To begin with, it is not at all clear what can be meant by saying that something is real as an appearance. If it is interpreted as meaning that the thing only appears to be real, then we have to conclude without qualification that it is not real. If what is meant is that the thing really appears, then we have to conclude without qualification that it is real, though here we may allow for the possibility of its appearing under some disguise. In neither case is any provison made for any half-way stage. But these are the only natural interpretations of the curious expression 'real as an appearance' and we are not given any other.

Moreover the ground which philosophers like Bradley advance for saying that space and time and matter are not ultimately real is that the ordinary notions of a material object or of things standing in spatial or temporal relations to each other are self-contradictory. But if a concept is self-contradictory, it is hard to see how anything could even appear to fall under it, let alone really fall under it as an appearance. A man who is older than another may look younger, but how could he be said to look both older and younger? What should we understand by this? Perhaps, that he looked older in some respects and younger in others; but then we are interpreting the description so that it ceases to be contradictory. So long as a description is contradictory it necessarily applies to nothing and nothing can even seem to satisfy it, for the sufficient reason that there is nothing in such a case which the delusive appearance can be taken to fall short of. If it really were self-contradictory to speak of things as being temporally related then there would be no possible state of affairs which talk of this kind would represent, and therefore nothing that events which merely appeared to be in temporal relation would be counterfeiting. The most that could be claimed would be that real things had properties which caused us to catetorize them in self-contradictory ways; but it would be highly misleading to translate this into the assertion that their appearances were self-contradictory: and even if this translation were allowed to pass, it would entail the conclusion not that such appearances were real at their own level but rather that they were not real in any sense at all.

This thesis is so obviously untenable that it is tempting to assume that its proponents were using words like 'real' and 'self-contradictory' in peculiar senses of their own. But the trouble with this suggestion is that the arguments which they bring against the world of appearances purport to be logical; they are designed to show that the categories under which we try to order it are self-contradictory in the normal sense. And while they do tend to use the word 'real' in a rather elastic fashion, so that sometimes a thing is said by them to be unreal when all that seems to be meant is that it is limited or relatively unimportant, nevertheless they do pass from the premiss that appearances are not ultimately real to the conclusion that the descriptions which are given of them are not true, or at any rate not wholly true: and this would indicate that in this context at least they also intended the word 'real' to be understood in something like a normal sense. The notion of degrees of truth is again an escape clause to which no evident meaning is attached.

It would seem then, that the attempts of metaphysicians of this kind to make the best of both worlds, to return with one hand at least part of what they have taken away with the other, have only led them into trouble. They would have done better to accept the conclusion that their views were quite irreconcilable with common sense, and not put themselves to dubious shifts in a vain attempt to save the appearances. They would indeed still be under some obligation to explain how we all can come to be so grievously mistaken; but if the appearances really are contradictory they are not worth saving.

Let us then suppose that we have to deal with a metaphysician who takes this more resolute attitude. His position, which has in fact been held at least by some oriental thinkers, is that the concepts of space and time and matter do not apply to anything at all. With or without argument, he maintains that reality falls under concepts of a totally different kind from these. How could he be refuted?

Well again he is exposed to the objection that if his view were true, he could not hold it, since he himself would not exist. But while this is enough to make the man appear riduculous, it does not strictly demolish his opinion. For logically the opinion might be true, even though it entailed that nobody could exist to hold it. In practice the proponents of these views invariably fall into contradiction by advancing them as views of their own or implying that other people are in error. For example they speak of the common sense view of the world as a popular delusion, which it cannot possibly be if there are no people to be deluded by it. But with sufficient care these contradictions can be avoided.

At this point many people would be content to say that any view of this kind is palpably false, and this in effect was the position which Moore took, though he reached it indirectly. His contention was that he knew for certain the truth of such propositions as that he had a body and that this body was frequently in contact with the surface of the earth and that the earth had existed for many years past, and since such propositions all implied the reality of space and time and matter it followed that if he really knew them to be true, any propositions which denied the reality of space and time and matter must be false.

This argument is perfectly rigorous. If its premisses are true, its conclusion must also be true. And no doubt the premisses are true. No doubt Moore did know many propositions of the type which I have just mentioned and no doubt each one of us knows many similar propositions about himself and his environment. Nevertheless it looks like a weakness in Moore's position, as he himself acknowledged, that he does not explain how we know these things; he does not show us how we are to vindicate these claims to knowledge. The answer to this may be that while there are many propositions which we could not reasonably claim to know unless we knew others which we could not reasonably claim to know unless we knew others which supported them, there must be some that are known immediately, if we are not to be saddled with an infinite regress; and a case might be made out for saying that Moore's examples belong to this primitive class. Even so, the metaphysician against whom this argument is directed might not think it difficult to counter. To what would seem to him an entirely dogmatic objection he might make an equally dogmatic rejoinder. He might say that since his own theory is true it follows that these common sense propositions are false and *a fortiori* that nobody knows them.

There is, however, a further argument on which it seems to me that Moore tacitly relies though I do not know that he ever made it explicit. What makes us so sure that there are physical objects which stand to one another in spatio-temporal relations is that it seems to us that we perceive them. We have sense-experiences which we take as establishing the truth of such propositions as that there is a chair over here and a book-case over there and a table in between them, or that the sun came out just after the rain had stopped. Now the question is raised whether our experiences can ever establish propositions of these kinds. But, so the argument runs, it just is in the nature of these propositions, it is characteristic of the meaning of the sentences which serve to express them, that they *are* established by those sorts of experiences. The rules which govern the use of sentences of this type are such as to correlate them with observable states of affairs; we understand the sentences when we know what observations would verify or falsify the propositions which they express. On certain occasions, indeed, we may have reasons for distrusting what appear to be such observations; we may have grounds for thinking that the appearances are deceptive in one way or another. But in default of any such special reasons for mistrust, to have what appear to be the appropriate experiences and to refuse to accept the proposition which is expressed by the sentence with which they are conventionally correlated is simply to violate the canons of the language which one purports to be using. In short, there are accepted criteria for deciding in particular cases whether these common sense propositions are true or false, and the question whether these criteria are satisfied in any given instance is a question not for philosophical argument but simply for empirical observation.

It is easy to see that this argument can be generalized, and also that when it is generalized it naturally leads to the conclusion that the only positive contribution that philosophy can make to knowledge is in the field of analysis. This position was not formally held by Moore himself, but it is implied in his practice and was explicitly adopted by most of his followers. For it is true not only of the propositions of common sense that there are recognized criteria for deciding when they are true or false. This applies equally to the technical theories and hypotheses of science and, though in their case the criteria are not empirical, to the <u>a priori</u> propositions of logic and pure mathematics. In these domains also there are recognized standards of proof and recognized procedures for determining whether these standards have been met. If someone refuses to regard a favourable experiment as confirming a scientific theory, then unless he has some special reason for mistrusting the experiment, unless he has grounds for suspecting that there has been an error of observation, or that there is some other special reason why the apparent result of this experiment is not to be taken at its face value, he simply has not understood what the theory is. If someone refuses to accept the result of a logical or mathematical demonstration, without having any special reason for thinking that the procedure which was employed in this instance was faulty or incorrectly carried out, he simply does not understand how logic and mathematics work.

The upshot of this is that the truth or falsehood of these propositions is not even a matter for philosophical discussion. It depends only on the satisfaction of the appropriate criteria; and whether the criteria are satisfied is a matter of empirical or formal fact. There is no place here for philosophy to intervene. But what then is there left for it to do? The official answer is, as I have indicated, that while it is not equipped to estimate the truth or falsehood of these propositions, it can and should attempt to elucidate their meaning; it should devote itself exclusively to the task of analysis. Exactly what is analysed, whether words or concepts, sentences or propositions or facts, how the analysis proceeds, what purpose it serves, and how its results are to be assessed are all matters of dispute. No very general agreement has been reached on any of them. There is just the feeling that philosophy must after all be good for something, and that the avenue of analysis, whatever that may be, is the only one left open to it.

But now let us look a little more closely at the argument which leads to this result. At first sight it is very persuasive. How could a philosophical discussion contrive to show that, in these perfectly normal circumstances, I am mistaken in believing in the existence of the physical objects which I can see around me? Of course I may fail to identify all of them correctly; it is conceivable even that I am the victim of some more serious illusion. But then there are ways of finding out whether this is so; and if they show that nothing is amiss, the question is settled. It would be merely neurotic to embark on an endless series of further tests, when one had no reason at all to expect that they would yield any different result. Theoretically, we may have to admit the possibility of our being deceived by our senses in any given instance, but to suppose that they invariably deceived us would be nonsensical. We can only attach meaning to the statement that our perceptions are sometimes delusive because we contrast them with the normal case in which they are veridical.

So far, so good. But now let us suppose that someone has been convinced by Berkeley that the things which he perceives are not material objects, as we understand the term, but only collections of ideas in his own mind.

How would this argument serve to disabuse him? The answer is that it would not serve at all. There will never be an occasion on which we can show him that because of his fidelity to Berkeley his judgements of perception run counter to the evidence. In the relevant circumstances, he will be as ready as we are to admit the clock has just struck four. Of course he interprets them differently; he does not think that they commit him to holding that these objects exist when he is not perceiving them, except perhaps as permanent possibilities of sensation, or as ideas in the mind of another person, or in the mind of God; but this does not mean that we can expect his judgement to dissent from ours in any concrete situation. We may say that he misunderstands these propositions, but if this is his mistake, it is not one that has any practical consequences.

But is it even obvious that he does misunderstand them? It might indeed be argued that this example exhibits not the weakness but the strength of Moore's position, on the ground that what is in dispute between the follower of Berkeley and ourselves is not the truth of any common sense propositions, but merely their analysis. His contention is that what I really mean when I say that this is a piece of paper is that I am having an idea, that is, a sense impression of a certain sort, which is linked in certain ways with other ideas: and the way to refute him would be to show that this is not what one ordinarily means when one makes a statement of this kind. He misunderstands these propositions, not in the sense that he does not know when to accept or reject them, but rather in the sense that he gives a false account of what they mean.

There is a good deal of support for this interpretation in Berkeley's own writings, but surely it does him an injustice. For if he really were contending that what is ordinarily meant by a physical object is a collection of ideas, it would be all too obvious that he was wrong. When the ordinary man speaks of a chair or a clock or a piece of paper, he plainly does so with the implication that these things exist unperceived. Perhaps he ought not to, but that is another question. There is no doubt that he does. This is the common sense view and Berkeley is not analysing but attacking it. He is not elucidating the way in which we systematize our experiences: he is putting up a rival system.

But how is this possible? How can the common sense view of the world be open to attack" In trying to answer this, we shall again find it helpful to draw upon Carnap's distinction between what he calls internal and external questions. The salient feature of Moore's technique is that it treats metaphysical questions internally, as though they arose within the framework of common sense. It is in this way that he refutes the metaphysician who makes the outrageous claim that time is unreal, by giving impeccable examples of events which occur in time. It is in this way that he proved the existence of external objects, simply by holding up his own two hands.[1] On these terms, his victory is complete; there is nothing more to be said. Even so the metaphysician feels that his position, so far from being overthrown, has not even been considered: and fundamentally he is right; the victory has been won on the wrong terrain. To say this is not to detract from Moore's achievement. He did more than anyone to dispel the cobwebs which prevented all of us, and not least the metaphysicians themselves, from seeing what they were about. Even so he misinterpreted them: for if anything is now clear, it is that metaphysical questions are external.

But this only gets us a little further forward. We still have to explain, much more precisely, what external questions are and also why anyone should wish to raise them. Why, to continue with our example, was Berkeley dissatisfied with the conception of the physical world which, whether he admitted it or not, is in fact the outlook of common sense? Why did he want to disallow the criteria in terms of which we are able to say with confidence and truth that things exist unperceived? Was it simply a matter of caprice? Did he have a psychological need to look at the world, or to speak about the world, in a different way? Was he trying to elaborate a conceptual system which would prove more useful to us than the system of common sense?

None of these is quite the correct answer. I do not deny that a philosopher may have psychological reasons, most probably unknown to himself, for mounting an attack against certain concepts, or that it would be of interest to discover what these reasons were. But this still would not explain to us what the philosopher was doing. For this we need to look at his actual procedure, to study the way in which he comes by his conclusions. And here the clue to the problem is that he reaches them by argument. The typical metaphysician does not simply say: I do not like the idea of matter, or motion, or time, or numbers, or individuals, or universals, or propositions, or negative facts, or whatever else may be in question; let us see if we cannot get along without it. He gives reasons for holding that these things do not exist.

These reasons mainly take two different forms. One common line of argument is that the category in question is not ultimate; the things which fall under it have been mistakenly hypostatized; what really exists is something else. This leads to such assertions as that there are no material things but only sense-data, no numbers but only numerals, no universals but only sets of similar particulars, or alternatively no particulars but only sets of compresent universals, no propositions but only sentences, no mental events but only dispositions to behave in certain ways, and so forth. If the philosopher who takes this line is of an analytical rather than a metaphysical turn of mind, he will prefer to say, for example, that material things are logical constructions out of sense-data, or that numbers are reducible to numerals, rather than that material things or numbers do not exist, but this is only a difference of formulation. This motive for trying to get rid of these sets of entities may be that they do not fit in with a preconceived idea of what the world is really like: especially among analytical philosophers the tendency is to eliminate the abstract in favour of the concrete, but it may also go the other way. Or it may be just that certain types of entity, like numbers or universals, strike one as mysterious, and one wishes to explain them in terms of other sorts of entities which one finds less problematic. Epistemological considerations also play their part. If it is believed that one type of entity is accessible only through another, as, for example, it has been held that we can have no acquaintance with material things except through apprehending sense-date, or no acquaintance with propositions except through understanding sentences, then there may be an inclination to try to reduce the more remote entities to those which give us access to them. The vindication of these claims is that the entities whose removal is desired should be successfully explained away. But the trouble here is that we are not always given clear enough criteria for deciding when a successful explanation of this sort has been achieved.

The second line of argument is that the category, or concept, which is put in question, is somehow defective. A standard of intelligibility is set up which it is then argued that it fails to satisfy. This is the nerve of Parmenides' attack on the concept of plurality, or that of the neo-Hegelians on the categories of space and time, or Ryle's on the concept of mind. Very often this line of argument is blended with the other. Thus Berkeley's reason for denying the existence of matter is principally that it is not verifiable. He takes over from Locke the requirement that for a concept to be intelligible it must refer to what could be experienced, and he argues that the physicist's conception of matter does not satisfy it. What we do experience, in his view, are what he calls sensible ideas, which correspond closely enough to what contemporary philosophers call sense-date; and he thinks it plainly contradictory to say of them that they exist when not perceived. At the same time, he maintains that any legitimate purpose which the conception of matter was designed to serve can be adequately fulfilled by talking only of immaterial percipients and their ideas. So he combines the view that the conception of matter is radically defective with the view that a different set of concepts, which are free from its defects, can be shown to be capable of replacing it. This is rather perplexing to his expositors, who are left in doubt whether to say that he rejected the concept of matter or merely offered an analysis of it. As we shall see in a moment, this distinction is somewhat arbitrary, but the points on which it turns are important.

In any case, whatever one may choose to say of Berkeley, the general aim of this second line of argument is to disqualify the concepts against which it is directed. But this brings us back to the question with which we started. How can there be any hope of disqualifying a concept of which it is obvious that we make successful use? If it is a plain matter of fact that a concept has empirical application, then how can one think that it is radically defective, that it is meaningless or contradictory? Surely the metaphysician can proceed only by shutting his eyes to what he knows to be true.

This is again Moore's argument, and if the metaphysician's questions were internal, in Carnap's sense, it would be decisive. But once it is seen that these questions are external, it loses a good deal of its force. For now we have to distinguish between the practical operation of a concept and the theory which it carries with it. This distinction is not sharp, since it is arguable that the description of any phenomena incorporates some element of theory, but it can be made sharp enough for our present purpose. Thus there is a sense in which the concept of possession by evil spirits had empirical application. There were criteria for deciding when a person was so possessed; the malady had characteristic symptoms which differentiated it from any other: there was no doubt that these symptoms did occur. At a time when the belief in good and evil spirits was part of popular culture, to deny the possibility of demonic possession might have seemed to be flying in the face of common sense. Nevertheless we now find it perfectly easy to dissociate this concept from the phenomena to which it was taken to apply. We can dismiss the very notion of evil spirits as nonsensical, and still do justice to the facts which sustained it. We simply account for them in a very different sort of way.

But surely the notion of matter is not on a level with that of evil spirits. There is, indeed, an important difference in that it is very much more difficult in this case to distinguish between fact and theory. It is not at all clear that we can give an adequate description of the facts without bringing in the notion of matter. The notion of a sensible idea which Berkeley takes as primitive is itself problematic; and his notion of the immaterial subjects who are presented with these ideas may well be contradictory. Nevertheless it has not been shown to be impossible to construct a 'language of appearance' in which the empirical data would be described in such a way as not to presuppose the existence, or indeed the non-existence, of either minds or matter. This was indeed the aim of William James and, after him, of Bertrand Russell in developing their theories of Neutral Monism, and though they did not fully succeed in carrying it through, I see no reason in principle why it should not be feasible. In that case, the introduction of the concept of persistent physical objects, the existence of which is independent of their being perceived, may be represented as one means among others of systematizing our experiences. If, pace Berkeley, it still appears to us as the only genuine possibility, this is because we cannot conceive of any other procedure which would come anywhere near to matching it in efficiency.

If one holds an operational theory about the significance of concepts, one will attach no importance to the difference between rival conceptual systems, so long as they can equally be made to square with the facts; indeed one will be inclined to say that there really is no difference between them. From this point of view, even such a concept as that of possession by evil spirits should not be regarded as illegitimate if there are genuine phenomena to which it is used to apply. The only mistake that can be attributed to those who employed it is that of supposing that they were doing something more than merely describing the phenomena: they did not realize that all that they really meant by saying that people were possessed by evil spirits was just that they exhibited such and such symptoms. In the same way Berkeley was, from this point of view, mistaken in thinking that he was refuting the advocates of matter. For since they allowed that the statements which they made about physical objects were verified only by the existence of the observable state of affairs, which for Berkeley consisted in the perception of sensible ideas, this is all that they could really have been referring to. If Berkeley was right in his contentions, the only mistake which he could attribute to his adversaries was that of failing to see that when they talked about matter they really were talking about sensible ideas.

It is, however, debatable whether we ought to equate the meaning of concepts, in quite this straightforward fashion, with the states of affairs to which they are understood to apply. Perhaps it is not of very great importance what meaning we decide to attach to the

rather vague word 'meaning', but it would be a mistake
to insist on cutting concepts off entirely from their
theoretical background. We are in something of a dilemma here because we want to reject a way of looking
at the world which seems to us absurd or even unintel-
ligible, but at the same time we do not want to say that
everything which is asserted by those who take this
point of view is false. Thus if the members of a primitive tribe attribute every natural occurrence to the
moods of Mumbo Jumbo, we may have no doubt that they are
utterly deluded: nevertheless we do not want to deny
their ability to detect that it is raining, even though
they see the rain as the expression of Mumbo Jumbo's
grief. Accordingly, we distinguish the fact which they
apprehend as well as we do from the ridiculous explanation which they give of it; and then if we are very
tough minded we may go on to say that all that they
really mean by their talk of Mumbo Jumbo's grief, though
of course they do not know it, is just that it is raining. But any anthropologist will regard this, rightly,
as a serious misrepresentation. We are imposing on them
a distinction which it could never occur to them to
make.

  As we have already seen in the case of Berkeley,
the way we react to this dilemma will very largely determine the view which we take of philosophical analysis. A very clear illustration of this is to be found
in Hume's theory of causation. Hume demonstrated incontrovertibly that the relation of necessity which is supposed to obtain between cause and effect cannot be a
logical relation, and he also saw that the idea that
distinct events were somehow glued together by a relation of non-logical necessity was an empty fiction:
it did not correspond to anything that one could conceivably observe. Accordingly, he placed the source
of the supposed necessity in our mental habits of as-
sociation, and for all practical purposes equated causality with regular sequence. Though his theory is open
to objection on some points of detail, I have no doubt
that on the central issues it is entirely right. But
if we accept the theory, at least in its essentials, do
we say that Hume has shown us what we really meant by
causality was defective and shown us the way to replace
it with something better? The reason against saying
that the concept on which Hume set to work turned out to

be defective is that we do not want to imply that it had
no application; we certainly do not want to say that the
world had to wait for Hume's theory before anyone was
capable of making a true causal statement. And if we
think along these lines, we shall be inclined to say
that what Hume did was to make clear to us what we really meant all along; we shall look upon his achievement as
a successful piece of philosophical analysis. On the
other hand, there is a very good sense in which the concept which emerges from Hume's analysis is not the same
as the popular notion which he set out to examine. It
may do the same work, but it does not keep the same
theoretical company. The popular notion was found to
be infected with incoherent ideas of power and agency;
and the fact that disinfecting it makes little or no
practical difference does not, I think, entitle us to
say that it makes no difference at all. In the same
way, I suppose it could be maintained that the account
which Einstein gave of simultaneity in his Theory of
Relativity only revealed to us what we had really meant
by the term all along: but it would in this case seem
much more accurate to say that he replaced a defective
concept with a better one. Yet once more we certainly
do not want to hold that until Einstein produced his
theory, no one ever judged truly that one event was
simultaneous with another.

  It appears from these examples that it is a fairly
arbitrary question whether we are to regard the results
of philosophical analyses as correcting our misappre-
hensions about the meaning of concepts, which are taken
to be in good order because we employ them successfully,
or as pointing out defects in the concepts themselves
and thereby leading us to modify them.. The salient
point is that it is shown to be possible for a concept
to be successfully applied even though it is embedded
in a theory which does not withstand critical scrutiny.
It follows that it is not automatically absurd for a
metaphysician to condemn a concept which is in common
use; he may indeed just be muddled, he may simply be
talking nonsense, but he may be making a valid criticism
of its theoretical background.

  But while this sort of apology for metaphysics may
cover philosophers like Berkeley and Hume whom we can
regard as offering us an alternative way of representing

the facts, which they believe, rightly or wrongly, to
be superior to the conceptual machinery of common sense,
it is harder to see how it applies to the more thorough-
going metaphysicians who simply dismiss the concepts of
space and time or motion or matter as self-contradictory
and then make a bee line for the Absolute. In their
case the impression given is not that they are offering
us an alternative way of representing the facts but
rather that they are altogether making light of them.

Here again, however, it will repay us to turn aside
from the strange conclusions which these metaphysicians
reach, and concentrate instead upon the arguments by
which they reach them. How, for example, does Zeno
prove that Achilles can never catch the tortoise? By
pointing out that when Achilles reaches the point from
which the tortoise started, the tortoise will have advanced some distance, however small, and that by the
time Achilles has covered that distance the tortoise
will have gone a little further and so ad infinitum.
How does McTaggart prove that time is unreal? By pointing out that the characteristics of being past, present
and future which every event is supposed to possess are
mutually incompatible, so that if we are to avoid a contradiction we must assume that events possess them at
different moments. So let us say that every event is
past at a present or future moment, present at a present
moment and future at a present or past moment. But then
the same difficulty arises with respect to the moments.
So either we relapse into contradiction or we are
launched upon an infinite regress.

Now both these pieces of reasoning, given their
premisses, are perfectly sound. If in order to traverse
any given distance one had to occupy each member in turn
of the infinite series of its parts, Achilles could not
catch the tortoise, indeed he could not move at all,
since he could never get started. If being past, present and future were non-relational characteristics of
events or moments, their attributions to either would
be logically vicious. Even so, we are disposed to say,
all that this proves is that these conceptions of the
nature of time and motion are mistaken, not that time
and motion are unreal. But the problem for our metaphysicians was that they did not see how these consequences were to be avoided; they did not see what other

account of time or motion could be given. And in this they were not so greatly to blame. It was only in the ninteenth century that mathematicians developed an adequate theory of continuity and even to this day there is disagreement about the way in which Zeno's arguments can most effectively be answered. Neither is there anything approaching unanimity among philosophers about the correct analysis of the passage of time. In my own view, the relation of temporal priority has to be taken as fundamental, and past, present and future defined in terms of it by reference to the temporal position of the speaker, this position itself being characterized by its temporal relation to other arbitrarily chosen events. But to a certain extent this vindicates McTaggart: for it leads to a 'static' spatial picture of the Universe as a four-dimensional continuum.

If we follow this approach, I think that we can even make sense of the metaphysical doctrine that things which are ultimately unreal are nevertheless real as appearances. We have seen that when this sort of talk is taken literally it can easily be made to seem ridiculous; the metaphysician is forced into the impossible position of maintaining both that some concept is self-contradictory and that it has application. But the explanation is, I suggest, that he is reacting in the same way to our ordinary system of beliefs as I supposed in my example that the anthropologist would react to the talk of the believers in Mumbo Jumbo. He would regard the idea of Mumbo Jumbo's grieving as nonsensical, but recognize that in their system it did correspond to a fact, namely the fact that he would describe by saying that it was raining. Similarly a metaphysician, like Bradley, wants to hold that our talk of space and time and matter is confused to the point of being implicitly self-contradictory and yet that it is an attempt to deal with the genuine phenomena. Of course he cannot consistently allow that the phenomena, even just *qua* phenomena, are spatio-temporally ordered, any more than the anthropologist could consistently allow that Mumbo Jumbo was apparently crying; what they can both say is that these are misguided attempts to describe genuine facts. But here the parallel ends, to the grave disadvantage of the metaphysician. For whereas the anthropologist has an alternative way of describing the facts, which is not exposed to the same objections, a metaphysician like

Bradley has not. He may assume that if *per impossibile* he were in the position of the Absolute he would have an entirely lucid view of everything that there is, but on his own showing he is not in this position, and never could be; and neither could we. So, having to his own satisfaction undermined our ordinary way of looking at the world, he not only leaves us with nothing to put in its place but also leaves himself with no firm standpoint from which to launch his attack. If our world collapses, he collapses with it.

In citing Bradley, I have taken an extreme case. There are metaphysicians, like Leibniz, who do offer us alternative conceptual frameworks. But the difficulty here is that it is not always clear how our observations are to be fitted into them. It may be that Leibniz's aim was fundamentally not so very different from that of Berkeley, in spite of the divergences in their outlook, but whereas I think I understand pretty well how Berkeley wanted us to conceive the world and why he believed that his system did greater justice to the phenomena, I cannot envisage what it would be like to conceive of the things around me as colonies of monads. Perhaps the analogy which Leibniz himself would have preferred is with a scientific theory of fundamental particles. But then, if the analogy is to be more than superficial, it has to be shown that this way of conceiving things is scientifically fruitful. I think this would be hard to accomplish, but I do not want to say *a priori* that it is impossible.

It has recently become the fashion to claim in defence of metaphysics that even though it does not yield us any knowledge, in the sense of establishing true propositions, it can afford us valuable insights. It is, however, not very easy to see what these insights can be, or why they are valuable, if they are not expressible as truths. Perhaps what is meant is that it is illuminating to be made to look at the world in a radically different fashion from that to which we are accustomed, and with this I agree, provided that the alternative way of looking at the world can be shown to be viable. But this is a large proviso and I do not know of any metaphysical system in which it is adequately met. Even so, it does not follow that the labour of those who have constructed these systems has entirely gone for nothing. As I see it, the main service which they perform for us is to induce us to look critically at the theoretical background of the operations of science and of common sense. Puzzles are raised about the relation of subject and predicate, or the functioning of general terms, or the status of abstract entities, or the meaning of necessity, or the infinite divisibility of spatial and temporal extension, or the dualism of mind and matter, or about our justification for attributing experiences to other persons or believing in the existence of external objects. Except in the rare case where the problem has a scientific bearing, the solution of these puzzles will not increase our power to control our environment, or to predict the future course of events, but there is a sense in which it can add to our understanding of the world, by opening our eyes to the theoretical implications of the ways in which we describe it. I have no sovereign recipe for solving, or dissolving, philosophical puzzles, but in some cases at least I think that the solution may take the 'metaphysical' form of showing that some class of entities is eliminable, or that the character of some concept, or set of concepts, has been wrongly understood, or that some concept could with advantage be more sharply defined or in some way modified.

The fact that external questions can be raised allows us even to tolerate such metaphysical assertions as that it is we who bring time into the world. The implication is that reality is conditioned by our method of describing it and that it is open to us to decide what method to employ, so that in a certain sense we do not just discover but determine what the world is like. But here again if we are to speak of alternative methods of description, we have to make sure that they are viable, and it is hard to see how there could be any intelligible description of the world which did not include the category of time. Moreover it must not be forgotten that when we speak of ourselves as doing this or that we are already operating within a conceptual system. For what are _we_, if not physical bodies which occupy a position in space and time? But so long as we are operating within a conceptual system, we are committed to its criteria of reality; and then to say that we bring time into the world is to say that nothing happened before the appearance on earth of human beings, which is simply false, just as it is simply false, if one is operating within a system which makes provision for physical objects, to say that they do not exist when they are not perceived.

What the metaphysician would like to do is take up a position outside any conceptual system: but that is not possible. The most that he can hope to achieve is some modification of the prevailing climate; to find a way, for example, of eliminating singular terms or perhaps even to contrive to represent himself and the things around him as logical constructions out of their appearances. But if such a venture is even to be intelligible, let alone of any theoretical interest, it must have at least a rough correspondence to the way in which things are ordinarily conceived. Thus if a philosopher is to succeed not merely in involving us in logical or semantic or epistemological puzzles but in altering or sharpening our vision of the world, he cannot leave common sense too far behind him.

This does not mean, however, that he must tie himself strictly to its apron strings. The insistence that ordinary language is perfectly in order has been a very useful corrective to the wilder flights of metaphysical speculation but, if taken too literally, it can lead to our letting things go by which might profitablly be questioned and mobilizing in defence of what does not need defending. It is indeed better to tabulate the milestones along the highway of ordinary usage than to rhapsodize about Nothingness or the Essence of Man; but it would be a mistake to forgo the more imaginative kinds of conceptual exploration, merely because of the greater risk of getting lost. In philosophy, nothing should be absolutely sacrosanct: not even common sense.

---

1. See 'Proof of an External World', British Academy Lecture, 1939, Reprinted in G.E. Moore's <u>Philosophical Papers</u>, (1959).

X.   THE   VALUE   OF   PHILOSOPHY

J. DAVID NEWELL

   -Associate Professor of Philosophy and Director of Graduate Studies at Washington College.

We begin to philosophize in the midst of life itself and when we conclude we are still in its midst. Before we even hear the word 'philosophy' for the first time, most of us possess a view of the world which is commonsensical, whether we like to admit or not. It is not necessary to believe, with Thomas Reid, that those beliefs (or the capacity to acquire them) are the gift of heaven.1 Nor is it necessary to hold that we humans have a special intuitive faculty which enables us to apprehend them as self-evident truths. We do not even have to agree with Moore that we <u>know</u> such beliefs to be true and that we know them with absolute certainty.2 The fact is, some of these beliefs are likely to turn out to be false. We allow that such beliefs are almost always <u>held</u> to be true and indubitable, but whether they are true or not is, in each case, a matter to be investigated. The point is that each of us holds these beliefs <u>prior</u> to any philosophical investigations, and so philosophy must begin or take its starting-point in the common sense view of the world.

   The common sense view of the world, on the other hand, cannot withstand the slings and arrows of critical cross-examination for very long. Under the trained and skillful eye of the philosopher, common sense beliefs are sometimes shown to have certain deficiencies which are repugnant to the intelligent individual. Vagueness, confusion, ambiguity, and contradiction, are often brought to light through a careful, systematic, and thorough-going scrutiny of our common sense beliefs. Moreover, as Moore has pointed out, the beliefs of common sense do not serve to give us a completely consistent and coherent picture of the universe.[3] To achieve this completeness, we are sometimes tempted to supplement common sense with one or more quasi-philosophical beliefs, usually accepted "on faith." But a philosophical examination of these supplementary beliefs in relationship with common sense convictions will often reveal intellectual difficulties for the common man. For example, is the common sense belief that there is evil in the universe consistent with the quasi-philosophical belief that God is both benevolent and omnipotent? The pondering of such questions is almost certain to bring the ordinary man to the arena of philosophy.

In entering the world of philosophy, however, we do not thereby completely divest ourselves of the common sense view of the world. Most of our original convictions remain intact throughout our philosophical journey. As William James contended, common sense is a perfectly definite stage in our thinking, and the changes which occur therein are gradual and painstaking.[4] Herein lies the fundamental importance of common sense thinking for philosophy. As long as we cling to our former beliefs, basing our decisions and actions upon them, we have no business evolving philosophical doctrines which contradict, or even appear to contradict them. Reid, and Moore are certainly right about this. Philosophy itself has long insisted on the consistency and coherence of beliefs, and the philosopher himself has not always kept this in mind. It is not surprising that the philosophical solipsist, for example, in insisting that he cannot know that there are other sentient beings beside himself in the universe, should feel a bit ridiculous when he engages in the process of trying to convince others of his view.

This example raises an interesting question. When a philosophical belief is in conflict or contradicts a common sense belief, what are we to do? The solipsist might take William James to be suggesting that, since his philosophical belief serves one purpose and his common sense belief serves another, the two beliefs could be viewed instrumentally and held simultaneously.[5] This, however, would not be a fair reading of the James essay, and even if it were, it will not do as an answer to our question. If a clearly articulated proposition is logically imcompatible with another clearly articulated proposition, they cannot both be held to be true in the same sense at the same time by any rational individual. There is nothing special about the conflict between a common sense belief and a philosophical belief. We are required to apply standards of evidence and justification to all propositions, whether commonsensical or philosophical. If both propositions are on equal footing after an examination of the available evidence, we would be well-advised to suspend belief in both propositions until some new evidence is available.

When a common sense belief is submitted to the rigorous tests of critical scrutiny, adequate evidence, and the like, there is a sense in which it is no longer merely a common sense belief. We may say that a <u>pure</u> common sense belief is one that is held with much conviction to be most certainly true. The unreflective man holds most of his beliefs in this fashion. A <u>philosophical</u> common sense belief, however, is one which has survived the tests and measurements of sustained reflection and unbiased critical examination. If absolute certainty is an essential element in human knowledge, it might well be that none of our beliefs will measure up. But the conclusion that we don't know anything is one of those philosophical views which seems so silly to most people. Short of certitude, we have varying degrees of evidence and justification for our beliefs. Surely those with the greatest amount of evidential support are superior to those with the least amount. It follows, then, that a philosophically held common sense belief is superior to an unsupported and dogmatically held (pure) common sense belief.

This is not to say that philosophy has won the day over common sense. It is, rather, to say that philosophical common sense is superior to unphilosophical common sense. When philosophy itself reaches far beyond the concrete world, it often becomes poetic and visionary. In this function, as Ayer has pointed out, it can serve to bring new insights and perhaps an entirely new way of looking at things.[6] In itself, this visionary exploration is a good thing. But in the end, the philosopher must make his home in this world, along with the butcher, the baker, and the candlestick maker.

We also hasten to point out that pure or ordinary common sense does not win the day either. The common sense view, unrefined by the insights and techniques of philosophy offers an impoverished view of man and the world. Dogmatically held beliefs, unsupported by argument and evidence, should be transformed through philosophical reflection into justified beliefs wherever possible. It is not common sense, but philosophical common sense that appeals to us. We do not want to submit our beliefs to a vote of the masses, or to the untrained judgments of the illiterate. What we do want, however, is a philosophy of life which will make sense out of this world and the experiences we have as its inhabitants. We want a way of looking at life which does not involve an intellectual schizophrenia. It is only when we bring every belief under the careful investigative eye of philosophy, and when our philosophizing in turn, does not lose sight of its role as the handmaid of life, that we can avoid the discomforts and absurbities of a divided mind. We must learn to sail between the Scylla of unreasoned common sense and the Charybdis of philosophy divorced from the world of men and things.

Whether or not we are willing to sail this middle course may very well depend in part on our character and temperament, but it will also depend upon the view we take of the nature and value of philosophy. There may not be any easy way of defing philosophy itself. Any hard and fast definition of it that we offer will surely exclude some recognized philosophers, as well as some putative philosophical ideas. In the final analysis, it may be that the only way to come to an understanding of the nature of philosophy is through a sustained investigation of the wide assortment of recognized philosophical works, by authors who have been acclaimed as philosophers. This, of course, would be a long range affair and one that would be well worth the time and effort. But some idea as to the nature of philosophy is already presupposed in the selection of works or authors, so our investigation would to some extent be sort of biased. Moreover, one would have to first be convinced of the value of such a pursuit <u>before</u> engaging in it, and this cannot be achieved unless we have some idea as to the nature of our subject-matter.

In what follows, then, we will attempt two things. First we will present a sketch of the nature and function of philosophical thinking, and second, we will point out the potential value of engaging in such reflection.

a) <u>The Nature of Philosophy</u>: If we attend to the root meanings of the word 'philosophy,' we may define philosophy by saying that philosophy is the love of wisdom. But everyone loves wisdom, even if we are not exactly sure what it is, so this will hardly serve to distinguish philosophy from other pursuits. A more constructive approach might be to say that philosophy is that form of intellectual activity which brings us to a better understanding of the universe in which we live. While this might be a better way to begin to define philosophy, it is not very much more adequate than the 'love of wisdom' approach. For the natural sciences and the social sciences, as well as the various arts, can also claim to be contributing to our understanding of life and the world in which it is lived. How, then, are we to distinguish the knowledge and understanding which we get through a study of the natural sciences, the social sciences, and the other humanities from that which comes from philosophy?

A helpful response to this question might take the form of erecting a sort of pyramid of human beliefs. At the base of the pyramid are the unexamined and unreflective beliefs of common sense. These beliefs are after all a part of our understanding of things, as long as we hold them to be true. At the next level of the pyramid, we find the beliefs of the separate sciences and humanities. Physics, chemistry, biology, and the like, make an enormous contribution to our understanding of the physical or natural world in which we live on a day to day basis. Psychology, sociology, political science, etc., offer us insight into the social, political and psychological aspects of human behavior. Art, music, literature, <u>et</u> <u>al</u>, provide us with a deeper understanding of the creative and artistic dimensions of human experience. Each of these disciplines specializes in the pursuit of knowledge concerning some aspect or aspects of the world and our experience of it. To do their respective tasks well, each discipline must focus its time and energies on one specific area. The result is a high degree of specialization on the part of each of the separate areas. And, in spite of a modicum of interdisciplinary mutual interests, we find that there is a widespread general tendency of these investigations to operate in almost total unawareness of each other.

We are reminded, at this point, of the five blind men who went to examine an elephant. Each man grasped a different part of the elephant and concluded that it was a very different thing from what the other four were examining. To some extent, this fragmentation of human knowledge and understanding is both natural and unavoidable. It is natural because each discipline is investigating a different aspect of the whole--each has its own subject-matter. It is unavoidable because the limitations of human intelligence and the time it takes to achieve a mastery of each separate subject-matter. It would be unreasonable and naive to expect one person to acquire a complete understanding of the whole. If the natural scientist, then, is able to immerse himself fully in the investigation of some feature of our world, we will have to concede that he has done his job and done it well. Such isolated and piecemeal discoveries will presumably be brought to bear on the untutored beliefs of the plain man and will subsequently shape our vision of the universe and life--hopefully for the better. The natural sciences, the social sciences, and the humanities, then, contribute to our understanding of the world in which we live and the manner in which we live therein.

If we ask a physicist what makes falling objects fall, he will be likely to offer us an explanation in terms of mass, velocity, gravitational forces, and the like. If we ask a psychologist what makes a person commit a mass murder, he will no doubt try to account for such untoward behavior in terms of some theory of motivation or personality. But if we ask the physicist *why* the universe is so constructed that objects fall downward and not upward, he is apt to refer us to the philosopher. Similarly, if we ask the psychologist *why* human beings

are so constituted that they do or abstain from doing
certain things, he might venture some philosophical
theory of human nature or call in the philosopher to do
so. Questions about the nature of the universe or the
nature of man, when broadly formulated, appear to be on
a level beyond the range and interest of the scientific
specialist. Such questions are not factual in nature and
might be seen as moving us beyond the level of the separate arts and sciences in the pyramid of human understanding.

At this level, it is assumed that the arts and sciences have accomplished their tasks, but have left certain issues unresolved. The person whose interests
range beyond the parts in the direction of more general
issues is a person with philosophical interests or lean-
ings. There appears at this level in our pyramid such
subdivisions of philosophy as the philosophy of science,
the philosophy of social sciences, the philosophy of
mathematics, political philosophy, philosophy of law,
philosophy of education, philosophy of history, philosophy of art, philosophy of literature, philosophy of religion, and so on. Philosophy of science, for example,
examines methods, explanations, and assumptions of the
organized empirical sciences with a view to showing its
distictive features, establishing its credibility, and
assessing its findings as revelations of genuine knowledge about the universe. The general aim of these
philosophy of... inquiries is to deepen our grasp of the
disciple or disciplines in question, usually by offering
some sort of overview in terms of which we can interre-
late and perhaps coordinate the seemingly fragmented features of our experience.

Unhappily, specialization occurs at this level as
well. The philosopher of art may know very little about
philosophy of science and vice-versa. It is almost as
difficult for one person to be an expert in every area
of philosophy as it is for him to be an expert on all of
the sciences or all of the arts. Moreover, it is possible to develop philosophical theories at this level from
within the particular discipline itself. Thus, for example, the political scientist whose special interest is
in political theory is likely to overlap to some extent
with the work of the political philosopher. A course of
study in political theory offered by a political scien-

tist is apt to contain much of the same materials as a course in political philosophy offered by a member of the philosophy department--though the way in which such materials are dealt with is likely to differ in any two such courses. The difference might indeed be a function of the involvement of the philosopher at yet another level in our pyramid: the level of philosophy proper or technical philosophy.

Philosophy proper, as we shall call it, traditionally includes the consideration of the most general questions of all. There are three areas of inquiry in 'philosophy proper' usually designated as metaphysics, epistemology, and ethics. Logic is a formal study which is generally included in programs of philosophical study, but it is as much the province of mathematics as it is of philosophy. The history of philosophy is also something that philosophers study, but it includes metaphysical, epistemological and ethical issues--along with many of the issues raised in the subdivisions of philosophy mentioned above. Metaphysics might be characterized as the attempt to understand existence or reality in general. Epistemology is the investigation of the foundations, nature, and scope of human knowledge itself. It asks, in other words, how it is that we can know, what we can know, if indeed we can know at all. Normative ethics is the inquiry into the principles and theories concerning obligations or duties, as well as evaluations of good and evil. All three, metaphysics, epistemology, and ethics, provide insights and direction for thinking that is done in the subdivisions of philosophy and presumably, at the other levels of human understanding.

To sum up, we have suggested that a pyramid of beliefs can be imagined in which the untutored beliefs of common sense serve as a base. These beliefs are refined and altered by the investigations of the scientist, social scientist, etc.. As the questions we ask become less factual and more general we move upward on the pyramid to the level of philosophy. Philosophy as applied to particular areas stands beneath philosophy proper, which is concerned with the epistemological, metaphysical, and ethical. Philosophy, so defined, is the attempt to understand and evaluate our common sense-scientific view of the universe as we experience and under-

stand it. This does not mean that our philosophical
beliefs are higher or more important than our other
beliefs, but only that they are held at a different
level of interest and inquiry.

Certain conclusions present themselves immediately,
if we accept this view of the place of philosophy. One
thing is that philosophy, by and large, depends on the
natural sciences, the social sciences, and the humanities, for its primary data. Secondly, philosophy seeks
a consistent set of relationships with the beliefs of
science and common sense. Thirdly, philosophy which is
integrated with the whole of our knowledge and understanding cannot fly in the face of the accredited findings of the common sense-scientific view of the world.
Fourthly, coming as it does at the top of our pyramid,
philosophy represents a freedom of the intellect to range
over questions and provide new insights into the conceptual framework with which we operate in the other areas
of human inquiry. We started out by saying that philosophy is that form of intellectual activity which brings us
to a better understanding of the universe and life. We
can now say that, if the sciences and arts help us to understand the universe, it is philosophy which helps us to
understand and evaluate that understanding.

b) <u>The Value of Philosophy</u>: In asking about the
value of philosophy we are essentially asking why it
ought to be studied. This may seem to be a strange
question for a philosopher to be asking, but it is the
function of philosophy to question everything, including itself. Bertrand Russell, in <u>The Problems of Philosophy</u>, justifies such an inquiry by saying that

> It is the more necessary to consider this question,
> in view of the fact that many men, under the influence of science or of practical affairs, are inclined to doubt whether philosophy is anything better than innocent but useless trifling, hair-splitting distinctions, and controversies on matters concerning which knowledge is impossible.[7]

We hasten to add that the negative evaluation of philosophy to which Russell refers is largely the result
of a blanket endorsement of the common sense view of
the world. It becomes all the more important, then,

for those who allow the common sense view to be even provisionally legitimate to insist on the value of philosophical thinking.

Russell thinks that philosophy has direct value only for those who actually study it, though it may have indirect value for those whose lives are affected by those who study philosophy. Russell is no doubt right in maintaining that the value of philosophy is largely personal. The formal study of philosophy provides the individual with the skills of clear thinking and careful reasoning. It presents us with a wide variety of ways of viewing central questions and reflecting on possible answers. This process itself tends to liberate us from the narrow confines of provincial thinking that issues in dogmas, prejudices, and biases. It encourages the individual to see the interrelatedness of the many and varied beliefs which he holds. It can provide him with the instruments needed to eliminate conflicts, contradictions, and vagueness from his general view of things. In so doing, philosophy assumes the value of a coherent, rationally consistent, world-and-life view. This does not mean that the individual must have some sort of elaborate system of thought in terms of which every belief is justified. But it does mean that the beliefs which he actually embraces will be internally consistent, or at least not inconsistent. By encouraging us to reflect on the coherence of our beliefs, philosophy helps us to overcome the framentary nature of beliefs which are the result of the over-specializations mentioned earlier. So, while no single individual can hope to master the whole of human knowledge, each of us can hope to bring into coherence those beliefs which we as individuals in fact hold to be true.

In addition to being coherent, we may further require that our beliefs have a basis in the world as we experience it. The importance of including common sense beliefs in the pyramid described earlier is crucial here. If our philosophical principles and conclusions are made to cohere with the whole fabric of our thoughts and experiences, we will have a good chance of avoiding those philosophical flights of fantasy which in the end leave us feeling silly.

As human beings we seem to have a strong general

tendency to have definite answers to life's questions. The definiteness of the unexamined common sense view of the world holds out a temptation for us in this regard. The beliefs of common sense which we all hold initially are familiar to us and the security of embracing them is something we do not wish to relinquish. It is at this point that individual temperament comes into play. Those who revel in the security of dogmatically held everyday beliefs are apt to remain imprisoned in the limited confines of unreflective common sense. Those who by nature are given to reflection and contemplation, on the other hand, are likely to find the arena of philosophy attractive, even if less comfortable than the world of plain common sense.

Returning to Russell for a moment we may say, in agreement with him, that "the value of philosophy is, in fact, to be sought largely in its very uncertainty."[8] Philosophical questions are designed to generate doubt and encourage independent inquiry. Philosophical thinking tends to create a certain measure of confusion and intellectual unrest in us--at least initially. There is no blind acceptance of dogmatic and authoritarian pronouncements in philosophy. Even when a philosopher adopts a certain point of view, he must do so provisionally, with an open mind to the possibility that his philosophical conclusions may be erroneous. It is not at all clear that the infallibility and certainty we seek can be found in any area of human inquiry, but it is surely not found in philosophy.

This uncertainty need not make us timid and weak-willed individuals who are driven to inaction for fear of being wrong. In fact, philosophers have often been at the forefront of political and social activities of various kinds. Russell himself was active in passivistic protests, women's suffrage and nuclear disarmament. In this light, we could take issue with Russell's suggestion that the value of philosophy is only indirect for those who do not study it. The great plethora of current concerns about euthanasia, abortion, suicide, the problems of modern technology, etc., have enabled the philosopher to exercise a direct and sometimes dramatic effect on the course of human events. And while it is sometimes hard to assess the full value of such influences, it would seem to be clearly naive to say that it has been either indirect or insignificant. Thus, while the value of philosophy is clear at the individual level, it can hardly be limited to the purely personal. It is perhaps naive to hope that the bulk of humanity will eventually become more philosophical or even that all philosophers will become more attuned to the so-called ordinary affairs of man. But this naive hope holds the greatest promise for a world in which human understanding will be advanced and life as we know it will be enriched.

---

1. Thomas Reid, Intellectual Powers of Man, 7th ed., (Boston: Phillips, Sampson, and Company, 1857), p. 363.

2. G.E. Moore, "A Defence of Common Sense," in Philosophical Papers, (London: George Allen and Unwin Ltd., 1959), p. 32.

3. G.E. Moore, "What Is Philosophy?" in Some Main Problems of Philosophy, (New York: Collier Books, 1962), p. 13.

4. William James, "Pragmatism and Common Sense," in Pragmatism, (New York: Meridian Books, Inc., 1960), p. 120.

5. Ibid., p. 127.

6. A.J. Ayer, "Metaphysics and Common Sense," in W.E. Kennick and Morris Lazerowitz, eds., Metaphysics: Readings and Reappraisals, (Englewood Cliffs: Prentice-Hall, Inc., 1966), pp. 317-330.

7. Bertrand Russell, The Problems of Philosophy, New York: Oxford University Press, 1959), p. 153.

8. Ibid., p. 156

SELECTED BIBLIOGRAPHY

Ayer, A.J.. "Metaphysics and Common Sense." In Metaphysics: Reading and Reappraisals, pp. 317-330. Edited by W.E. Kennick and Morris Lazerowitz. Englewood Cliffs, N.J.: Prentice-Hall, Inc., 1966.

Joad, C.E.M.. Essays in Common Sense Philosophy. First Published 1920; reissued, Port Washington, N.Y.: Kennikat Press, 1969.

James, William. Pragmatism. New York: Longmans, Green, and Co., 1907; reissued ed., New York: David McKay Company, 1968.

Moore, G.E.. Philosophical Papers. London: George Allen & Unwin, Ltd., 1959.

_____. Some Main Problems of Philosophy. London: George Allen & Unwin Ltd., 1953.

Malcolm Norman. "Defending Common Sense." Philosophical Review, Vol. 58 (1949), pp. 201-220.

Rogers, A.K.. A Brief Introduction to Modern Philosophy. New York: The Macmillan Company, 1899.

Sidgwick, Henry. The Methods of Ethics. 7th ed. New York: Dover Publications, 1966.

_____. Lectures on the Philosophy of Kant and Other Philosophical Lectures & Essays. London: Macmillan and Co., 1905; reprint ed., New York: Kraus Reprint Co., 1968.

Woozley, A.D.. "Ordinary Language and Common Sense." Mind, Vol. 62 (July, 1953), pp. 301-312.

SUGGESTED ADDITIONAL READINGS

Broad, C.D.. The Mind and Its Place in Nature. Paterson, N.J.: Littlefield, Adams & Co., 1960.

_____. "A Reply to My Critics." In The Philosophy of C.D. Broad, pp. 803-805. Edited by P.A. Schilpp. New York: Harper & Row, 1959.

Campbell, C.A.. "Common Sense Propositions and Philosophical Paradoxes." PAS, Vol. 45 (1944-45) pp. 1-25.

Chisholm, Roderick. "Philosophers and Ordinary Language." Philosophical Review, Vol. 60 (1951) pp. 317-328

Duncan-Jones, A.E. and Ayer, A.J.. "Does Philosophy Analyze Common Sense?" PAS, Suppl., Vol. 16, (1937) pp. 139-176.

Edwards, Paul. "Common Consent Arguments for the Existence of God." In The Encyclopedia of Philosophy, Vol. 2, pp. 147-55. Edited by Paul Edwards. New York: Macmillan Publishing Company, 1967.

Grave, S.A.. The Scottish Philosophy of Common Sense. London: Oxford University Press, 1960.

_____. "Common Sense." In The Encyclopedia of Philosophy, Vol. 2, pp. 155-160. Edited by Paul Edwards. New York: Macmillan Publishing Company, 1967.

Jensen, Henning. "Common Sense and Common Language in Thomas Reid's Ethical Theory." Monist, Vol. 61 (April, 1978) pp.299-310.

Kneale, William. "Gilbert Ryle: 1900-1976." Arch. Phil., Vol. 40, (July, 1977) pp. 353-362.

Lee, Donald S.."Pragmatic Ultimates: Contexts and Common Sense." Southern Journal of Philosophy, Vol. 15 (Winter, 1977) pp. 493-503.

Malcolm, Norman, "Moore and Ordinary Language." pp. 600-675. In The Philosophy of G.E. Moore. Edited by P.A. Schilpp. Evanston and Chicago, 1942.

_____. "Moore and Wittgenstein on the Sense of 'I Know'." In Thought and Knowledge. Essays by Norman Malcolm. Ithaca: Cornell University Press, 1977, pp. 170-198.

Newell, J. David. "Sidgwick's Common Sense Realism." Philosophy Research Archives, Vol. 13, No. 2, (August, 1979).

Pierce, C.S. Collected Papers, Vol. V, pp. 293-313 and 346-375. Edited by Charles Hartshorne and Paul Weiss, 6 volumes, Cambridge, Mass. (1931-1935).

Pring, Richard. "Common Sense and Education." Proc. Phil. Educ. Soc., Vol. II (July, 1977) pp. 57-77.

Ross, Jacob Joshua. "Rationality and Common Sense." Philosophy, Vol. 53, (July, 1978) pp. 374-381.

Thomas, David. "Sociology and Common Sense." Inquiry, Vol. 21 (Spring, 1978) pp. 1-32.